ARMSTRONG'S
WAR

Angela

from Colleen

*with great affection
and respect*

Also by Colleen Murphy:

Beating Heart Cadaver
The December Man (L'homme de décembre)
The Goodnight Bird
The Piper

ARMSTRONG'S WAR

COLLEEN MURPHY

PLAYWRIGHTS CANADA PRESS | BANFF CENTRE PRESS
TORONTO | BANFF

Armstrong's War © Copyright 2014 by Colleen Murphy

PLAYWRIGHTS CANADA PRESS
202-269 Richmond St. W., Toronto, ON M5V 1X1
416.703.0013 ✦ info@playwrightscanada.com ✦ www.playwrightscanada.com

BANFF CENTRE PRESS
The Banff Centre, Box 1020, Banff, AB T1L 1H5
403.762.6408 ✦ press@banffcentre.ca ✦ www.banffcentrepress.ca

For professional or amateur production rights, please contact:
Michael Petrasek at The Talent House
204A St. George Street, Toronto, ON M5R 2N5
416.960.9686, michael@talenthouse.ca

We acknowledge the financial support of the Canada Council for the Arts, the Ontario Arts Council (OAC), the Ontario Media Development Corporation, and the Government of Canada through the Canada Book Fund for our publishing activities.

Jacket design by Kisscut Design
Book design by Blake Sproule

LIBRARY AND ARCHIVES CANADA CATALOGUING IN PUBLICATION
Murphy, Colleen, 1954-, author
    Armstrong's war / Colleen Murphy.

A play.
Issued in print and electronic formats.
ISBN 978-1-77091-248-9 (pbk.).--ISBN 978-1-77091-249-6 (pdf).--
ISBN 978-1-77091-250-2 (epub)

    I. Title.

PS8576.U615A86 2014   C812'.54   C2014-904097-0
                                               C2014-904098-9

First edition: September 2014
Printed and bound in Canada by Imprimerie Gauvin, Gatineau

for my son, August

PREFACE

Drama has always been a key component of The Banff Centre's programming. In its founding year of 1933, at the height of the Great Depression, a two-week program in drama was offered to 190 students. Only a few years later, in 1935, playwriting was officially added to the programs on offer. Because of this history, in preparation for the Centre's seventy-fifth year of continuous operation, it felt appropriate to commission a new play to celebrate the Centre's legacy of commitment to the arts and artists; a play that would illustrate the interests and concerns of playwrights in the early years of a new century. More than eighty submissions on a vast array of subjects were received from across Canada, and in April of 2008, Linda Gaboriau, Maureen Labonté, John Murrell, Brian Quirt, and Bob White joined me to select the recipient of the anniversary commission.

While the task was daunting given the overwhelming richness and quality of the proposed works, the terms of the commission helped to identify a clear favourite: Daniel MacIvor proposed a play that would be a departure for him as a playwright, larger in scope and scale than much of his previous work. *Arigato, Tokyo* was to be a play about a Canadian writer communicating with a new audience, challenging his understanding of human and cultural differences, and challenging himself as a man and as an artist on a global stage. It has evolved into a play that is exacting, intensely theatrical, and enormously human. It was a good match with the anniversary celebration and a unanimous choice for the jury.

Fortunately, and happily, the discussions and deliberations did not end there. Despite the breadth of subject matter among the submissions overall, several playwrights responded to Canada's involvement in the war in Afghanistan. Colleen Murphy proposed *Armstrong's War*, a play about the consequences of serving under combat conditions and focusing on a soldier's return to Canada. Hannah Moscovitch proposed *This is War*, a play about the immediate effects of battle on the men and women of our armed forces, but, like Colleen, her interest was much broader. Hannah's play also explores some of the messy human aspects of modern combat, from the difficulty of knowing the enemy to the psychological impact inflicted upon soldiers on the same side of the conflict.

These were powerful ideas advanced by gifted writers working within a genre that is underrepresented in theatrical literature in this country: the Canadian war play. It seems strange that the performing arts discourse around Canada as a nation at war is largely confined to the media and the political sphere. Enabling these writers to create and develop these plays would contribute to the conversation about Canada's role as a warrior nation within the public arena of the theatre.

And so it was that with a little budget juggling and creative schedule manoeuvring, the anniversary commission provided the opportunity for three plays to be created. With the active co-operation of the Banff Playwrights Colony, first directed by Maureen Labonté and now led by Brian Quirt, and with reading and workshop opportunities in Banff and Toronto, both *This is War* and *Arigato, Tokyo* have been produced in critically acclaimed premieres in Toronto, at the Tarragon Theatre and at Buddies in Bad Times Theatre, respectively (with more productions planned), while Colleen Murphy's *Armstrong's War* made its workshop premiere at Finborough Theatre in London, England, and debuted in Canada at the Arts Club Theatre Company in Vancouver.

We are thrilled to share these plays with you in partnership with our friends at Playwrights Canada Press, and look forward to many more opportunities to showcase the rich diversity of the dramatic arts in Canada.

Kelly Robinson
Director of Theatre Arts, The Banff Centre
2008–2013

Armstrong's War was staged in a workshop production, presented by Flying Bear Productions and ABG Productions in association with Neil McPherson, at Finborough Theatre in London, UK, from August 11 to 27, 2013, with the following cast and creative crew:

Halley Armstrong: Jessica Barden
Michael Armstrong: Mark Quartley

Director: Jennifer Bakst
Design: Philip Lindley
Lighting: Jack Weir
Costume design: Maud Dromgoole
Music: Angus MacRae

The play was first produced by the Arts Club Theatre at the Granville Island Stage, Vancouver, from October 17 to November 9, 2013, with the following cast and creative crew:

Halley Armstrong: Matreya Scarrwener
Michael Armstrong: Mik Byskov

Director: Mindy Parfitt
Set design: Naomi Sider
Costume design: Carmen Alatorre
Lighting design: Conor Moore
Sound design: Candelario Andrade

AUTHOR'S PRODUCTION NOTE

Use music sparingly at the beginning and end and subtlety when composing the score or soundscape for the transitions. Do not underscore the text.

CHARACTERS

Halley Armstrong, twelve
Corporal Michael Armstrong, twenty-one

SETTING

The play takes place in the rehabilitation wing of a hospital in Ottawa, Canada, from late February to mid April 2007.

SCENE ONE

The room is institutional with a swinging door and a side window. The single bed is messy, sheets hanging off the sides and touching the floor. A laptop sits on a night table, crutches and weights rest in one corner, an overflowing trash can in the other.

It is late afternoon and nearly dark outside.

MICHAEL is lying under the bed on a pile of wrinkled clothes. He wears sweatpants and a T-shirt—his feet are bare.

The swinging door is pushed open.

Enter HALLEY in a wheelchair. She's bundled up in winter clothes, boots, and has a packsack on her lap.

HALLEY:
Hello!

No response from MICHAEL.

Hello?

HALLEY turns around, pushes the door open, wheels out to check the room number, then wheels back into the room. She flicks on the light switch and looks around. She notices a foot sticking out from under the bed.

Are you Corporal Armstrong?

No response.

Hello?

No response.

Are you sleeping?

MICHAEL:
…no.

She wheels closer to him.

HALLEY:
Are you Corporal Armstrong?

MICHAEL:
…yeah.

HALLEY:
Sorry I'm late.

She puts on the brakes, pulls off her hat and mitts, and opens her parka.

MICHAEL:
Who are you?

HALLEY:
I'm Halley.

Underneath the jacket she wears a Pathfinder uniform—a green T-shirt and navy-blue sash covered with badges. She pulls a book from her pack.

I chose a book from the series Cordelia Hampstead—Girl Detective. This is *The Case of the Talking Skeleton.*

She begins to read quickly and with expression.

"Chapter One. Cordelia and her best friend, Allison, were on the bike trail when it began to drizzle. 'It's probably just a sun shower,' said Cordelia, eager to try out her new bicycle, but in a few moments it started to pour. Allison shouted, 'There's an old boathouse down there!' Swiftly the girls raced towards the river. They pushed the creaky door open and dragged their bikes inside. Then they heard something. 'Did you hear that?' whispered Allison. Cordelia listened to a man's squeaky voice coming from outside. 'Move it to another place or bury it.'"

MICHAEL:
...excuse me...

HALLEY:
(reads) "Then another voice said, 'Good idea, but we gotta wait till dark or someone might see.' And just then Allison opened her mouth and sneezed so loud Cordelia jumped."

MICHAEL:
Excuse me.

HALLEY:
(reads) "The voices stopped and they heard footsteps hitting the water then boots running, slapping against branches—"

MICHAEL:
HEY.

HALLEY:
...sorry?

MICHAEL:
Who are you?

HALLEY:
My name is Halley. I'm a Pathfinder.

MICHAEL:
…a pathfinder?

HALLEY:
Brownies are from ages seven to nine, Girl Guides from nine to eleven, Pathfinders from twelve to fourteen, and Rangers from fifteen to seventeen. I'm twelve so I'm a Pathfinder and I'm your reader for the next six weeks.

MICHAEL:
Do you have to read or can you not read?

HALLEY:
I'm an excellent reader. It's my favourite thing. My best friend Jackie calls me a reading fiend—a *fiend*. Once I read five books in twenty hours—three Cordelia Hampsteads and *A Great and Terrible Beauty* which I'd read before, and *Twilight* which I'm not supposed to read but I borrowed it from Clara. She's my older sister. I started reading each morning at eight a.m. and finished at eight p.m. minus one hour for lunch and dinner. It set a record in our house. My mom reads a lot, too, but mostly she reads romance—

MICHAEL:
Please stop.

He crawls out from under the bed and gets to his feet with some difficulty.

HALLEY:
Is something wrong? Are you in pain?

MICHAEL:
I don't want a reader.

HALLEY:
But you wrote your name on the Readers Wanted list.

MICHAEL:
I changed my mind.

HALLEY:

Oh.

MICHAEL:

Sorry.

HALLEY:

Before Christmas I was reading to a senior who had thick white hair. He asked me to read the Psalms, which are very strange and beautiful but then he had a diabetic incident and died before our third session.

MICHAEL:

Like I said—I'm sorry.

HALLEY:

It's not like I can earn badges for mountain climbing or swimming.

MICHAEL:

There's probably lots of people in here who'd be happy to have you read to them.

HALLEY:

All the people on the Readers Wanted list have been assigned to other readers. My enemy and fellow Pathfinder, Brittany MacDonald-Lapinski, is a reader for *three* people in this hospital—an elderly lady who had a heart operation, a kid with osteochondrodysplasias, and another kid with cancer.

MICHAEL:

Like I said—sorry.

HALLEY:

I picked you because we have the same last name.

MICHAEL:

I'm not in the mood today.

HALLEY:
If you're not in the mood for a story I can write letters for you to send to your girlfriend or to your parents or relatives. *(eagerly reaches into her pack)* I carry my laptop with me at all times.

MICHAEL:
Don't bother. I'm tired.

He limps over to the door and holds it open for her. She puts her hat on and starts to do up her parka—at some point her cellphone rings.

HALLEY:
It took me an hour and a half to get here—which didn't count having to sit outside in the freezing cold because the mobility bus was supposed to... sorry, I have to— *(into her phone)* I'm busy... yeah, no, I'm here... it was late but I got here—no, here at the hospital with the, yeah the soldier—yeah, yeah, the door's open... *(eyes rolling)* yeah... Mom, I have to go, I— Yeah okay, Mom—no, Mom, I'm fine, I'm fine, no I'm fine fine fine fine okay. *(to MICHAEL)* Sorry, I—like I was saying, the mobility bus was supposed to pick me up at four from the school but didn't come until four forty-five because of the snow then they had to pick up three other people along the way here!

MICHAEL:
Can't blame the snow on me.

HALLEY:
I'm not blaming the snow on—it's just, I don't know... I assumed soldiers had good manners but it's probably your pain that makes you rude—that's why I'm here—I'm here to help you temporarily escape the pain of your wounds by inviting your imagination into other worlds—

MICHAEL:
You got no business making assumptions about my pain.

HALLEY:

I'm not—I'm just... I'm making conclusions based on evidence: a) you're in a rehabilitation wing, b) you were lying under your bed, and c) you limp so you're probably recovering from a physical wound and you're suffering from post-traumatic stress disorder—

MICHAEL:

I don't have PTSD.

HALLEY:

Ms. Wren—she's my Pathfinder leader—she told me I should talk softly and be extra sympathetic because many soldiers come back from war with post-traumatic stress—

MICHAEL:

You talk too much.

HALLEY:

Okay—no more talking; I'll just read.

She opens the book, starts reading.

"Allison whispered, 'What are we going to do?' 'We're not staying here,' said Cordelia, taking the handles of her bike and heading outside. Allison followed as Cordelia walked around behind the boathouse to where the voices had come from. Allison was afraid, 'What if they're hiding and watching us right now?' 'Allison,' said Cordelia, trying to be tolerant of her friend's fear, 'It's important to get the facts... I just want to investigate the'—suddenly Cordelia stopped in her tracks—"

MICHAEL:

Okay, enough.

HALLEY:

It gets more exciting—

(*reads*) " 'Look down there near my foot,' whispered Cordelia. Allison looked down and saw it… a bone hand attached to a bone arm. Cordelia bent down. 'Don't touch it,' warned Allison, but Cordelia's fingers were already flicking away the sand… the arm was attached to a shoulder, to a spine, to a skull."

MICHAEL:
What's your name again?

HALLEY:
Halley *Armstrong*.

MICHAEL:
Stop reading, Halley Armstrong.

HALLEY:
Don't you like the story?

MICHAEL:
I'm too old for that kind of stuff.

HALLEY:
Oh… I have another book I'm currently reading…

HALLEY *searches in her pack.*

MICHAEL:
You got any war books in there?

HALLEY:
No, but… (*pulls out another book*) this one is more mature. Ever heard of Heathcliff?

MICHAEL:
No.

HALLEY:

(*opens the book*) You'll love this—this is literature, but instead of starting at the beginning I'm going to jump ahead to the exciting part. Now, all you need to know is that Catherine's in bed pregnant with Linton's child—at least I think it's Linton's child—Linton is her husband and, anyway, she's dying and her true love Heathcliff comes to visit...

(*reads passionately*) " 'Oh, Cathy! Oh, my life! How can I bear it?' was the first sentence he uttered, in a tone that did not seek to disguise his despair—"

MICHAEL:

I don't want to hear about Heathcliff or singing skeletons—

HALLEY:

Talking skeletons—

MICHAEL:

I don't want to be read to or talked to—I just want to sleep.

She closes the book.

HALLEY:

I bet the word "wren" makes you think of a delicate bird but Ms. Wren is a condor. She's not big or anything, in fact, she's tiny, but her personality takes up most of the sky. "A leader of women" she likes to call herself, but if I tell her I left early because you wanted to sleep she'll blame me and say I wasn't sensitive enough or I didn't have the right attitude, that I wasn't sufficiently prepared. I'm not afraid of her or anything but sometimes she's... sometimes I'm a little tiny bit afraid of her.

MICHAEL:

Is there a form I have to sign saying you completed your mission?

HALLEY:

Yes, but you can't sign it until we're finished all the reading sessions.

MICHAEL:

I probably won't be here next week.

HALLEY:

Why not?

MICHAEL:

Might get my discharge.

He slides under the bed.

HALLEY:

Where are you going?

No response.

Do you have a puppy under there or something?

MICHAEL:

You kids come in here with your bullshit compassion—let's pet a vet, help him or her escape their nightmares—people come in here from churches, from yoga centres, from grief counselling; they come and give me care packages, blankets, a laptop, and yeah, I was even given a puppy once, but I gave it back 'cause it's impossible to look after a puppy in a crowded place like this—you go out there you'll see a long line of people offering solace and pity and understanding, but their solace won't save me and their pity won't protect me and now, just when I get a few minutes of silence, you roll in here with your books and your imagination and go on about my pain—

HALLEY:

All I want to do is earn my Community Service badge.

MICHAEL:

You want a badge? I'll show you a badge.

He drags out a wrinkled uniform shirt with his regiment badge on it.

Take a close look. That's a badge: Canadian Armed Forces. That's a fuckin' badge.

HALLEY picks up her pack then swivels around towards the door.

HALLEY:
I know the F-word, too—and you know what else I know? There's no long line of people out there—there's hardly anyone around. When I tried to find someone to ask directions to your room—I couldn't find a single person in the hallways—it's like a ghost town in here.

Exit HALLEY.

MICHAEL:
Robbie... Robbie... shhh...

He reaches up and grabs a pillow from his bed, then slithers back under with the pillow.

...here, rest your head on this.

He smoothes out the pillow.

SCENE TWO

One week later. Same room. The lights are on.

It is late afternoon and getting dark outside.

MICHAEL is dozing under the bed still in his sweats—feet bare, the bed a mess. The pillow is on top of the bed.

Enter HALLEY, winter clothes over her uniform and holding a full packsack on her lap. She wheels close to him, lifts the packsack up high, then drops it on the floor, where it lands with a thud.

MICHAEL flinches.

MICHAEL:
What the hell?

HALLEY:
Books about war.

MICHAEL:
Go away.

HALLEY:
Mrs. Parker—she's the school librarian—*(coughs)* she helped me pick them out. There's a book on Vimy Ridge, one on Napoleon, battle of Stalingrad, World War I, Canadian heroes in WWI, Canadian heroes in WWII, War of 1812, American Civil War—

MICHAEL:
Told you last time I don't want a reader.

HALLEY:
We have five reading sessions left so I can read one of these to you or I can cheat by asking you to sign this paper now and for the rest of my life whenever I look at my Community Service badge I will know that I'm living a lie because I will have broken my Guiding Promise which is: *I promise to do my best, to be true to myself, to my faith, and to Canada; I will help others and accept the Guiding Law.* Do you know what the Guiding Law is?

MICHAEL:
No.

HALLEY:
To be honest and trustworthy, use my resources wisely, respect myself and others, to recognize and use my talents and abilities, protect our common environment, live with courage and strength, and share in the sisterhood of Guiding. Then I added my very own personal Guiding Law: *Stand tall.*

MICHAEL:
...fine. Pick one.

HALLEY:
You pick.

MICHAEL:
I don't care.

HALLEY:
Open it up and pick a book you'd like me to read.

After a long moment he crawls out from under the bed, reaches into her pack, and absently pulls out a book. He hands it to her.

You didn't even look at the title.

MICHAEL:

(*glances at the cover*) *The Red Badge of Courage*.

HALLEY:

Good choice—(*coughs*) I read it last year.

MICHAEL:

Have you read all these books?

HALLEY:

No, not all of them.

She takes off her mitts and hat and opens her jacket.

…are you ready?

MICHAEL:

If I fall asleep, don't wake me.

He sits on the bed and lies back.

HALLEY:

The Red Badge of Courage by Stephen Crane. Chapter One.

She begins to read with a pronounced Southern accent.

"The cold passed reluctantly from the earth, and the retiring fogs revealed an army stretched out on the hills, resting. As the landscape changed from brown to green, the army awakened and began to tremble with eagerness at the noise of rumours.

"Once a certain tall soldier developed virtues and went resolutely to wash a shirt. He came flying back from a brook waving his garment bannerlike.

" 'We're goin' t' move t'morrah—sure,' he said pompously to a group in the company street. 'We're goin' 'way up the river, cut across, an' come around in behint 'em.' "

MICHAEL:
These guys with the Confederate Army?

HALLEY:
No—the Union Army.

MICHAEL:
They sound like they're from Texas.

HALLEY:
I'm just following how the words are written and the punctuation.

MICHAEL:
You should talk like they're from Washington or Boston.

HALLEY:
Do you want to read?

MICHAEL:
No.

HALLEY:
We could take turns.

MICHAEL:
I'll just listen.

HALLEY continues to read.

HALLEY:
"There was a youthful private who listened with eager ears to the words of the tall soldier and to the varied comments of his comrades. After receiving

a fill of discussions concerning marches and attacks, he went to his hut and crawled through an intricate hole that served it as a door. He wished to be alone with some new thoughts that had lately come to him."

MICHAEL *suddenly looks under the bed.*

Are you going back to sleep?

MICHAEL:
No, just checking.

HALLEY:
I think you've got a hamster or a rabbit under there.

MICHAEL:
You gonna read or what?

HALLEY:
Mrs. Parker holds a Reading Circle in the library every day after class. There are five of us—four girls and one boy, Austin—and we sit in a circle and we each read a page and usually finish a novel in three weeks. It was Austin who chose this book last year. Did you know that Stephen Crane was only twenty-three when he wrote this?

MICHAEL:
That's only two years older than me.

She hands him the book.

HALLEY:
Mrs. Parker told us that this book has never been out of print. Why don't you read a page?

MICHAEL:
I don't like reading out loud.

HALLEY:
It's more fun if we take turns.

MICHAEL:
I'll try...

Reluctantly he takes the book.

HALLEY:
My dad always said that the word "try" is an escape route.

MICHAEL:
...here goes nothing...

(reads) "The youth was in a little trance of astonishment. So they were at last going to fight. On the morrow, perhaps, there would be a battle, and he would be in it."

"On the morrow"—I like that.

"He had, of course, dreamed of battles all his life—of vague and bloody conflicts that had thrilled him with their sweep and fire. In visions he had seen himself in many struggles. He had imagined people secure in the shadow of his eagle-eyed prowess. But awake he had regarded battles as crimson blotches on the pages of the past."

MICHAEL hands the book back to HALLEY.

HALLEY:
That was good.

(reads) "He had burned several times to enlist. Tales of great movements shook the land.

"One night, as he lay in bed, the winds had carried to him the clangoring of the church bell as some enthusiast jerked the rope frantically to tell the twisted news of a great battle… Later, he had gone down to his mother's room… 'Ma, I'm going to enlist.' 'Henry, don't you be a fool'… She had then covered her face with the quilt… Nevertheless, the next morning he had gone to a town that was near his mother's farm and had enlisted."

Your turn.

She hands the book to MICHAEL *and he takes it.*

MICHAEL:
(reads) "When he had returned home his mother was milking the brindle cow. Four others stood waiting. 'Ma, I've enlisted,' he had said to her diffidently. There was a short silence. 'The Lord's will be done, Henry,' she had finally replied, and had then continued to milk the brindle cow.

"When he had stood in the doorway with his soldier's clothes on his back, and with the light of excitement and expectancy in his eyes almost defeating the glow of regret for the home bonds, he had seen two tears leaving their trails on his mother's scarred cheeks."

MICHAEL *stops reading.*

Silence.

HALLEY:
Did you lose your place?

MICHAEL:
No.

HALLEY:
Ms. Wren warned me not to ask personal questions but can I ask you one?

MICHAEL:
Depends what.

HALLEY:

Does reading this make you sad?

MICHAEL:

No.

HALLEY:

What did your mother say when you told her you were joining the army?

MICHAEL:

At send-off she said she was proud of me... but I wasn't thinking about her just now; I was thinking about Robbie's mother.

HALLEY:

Who's Robbie?

MICHAEL:

...a friend of mine. Robbie flies around the room like a bird—he's everywhere at once.

HALLEY:

Wow. I wish my friend Jackie could be everywhere at once—it'd be a lot easier to spend time with her. We aren't talking right now because on Monday she called me "cumbersome." Do you know what that word means?

MICHAEL:

...sort of.

HALLEY:

It means "difficult to handle because of weight or bulk, troublesome or onerous." The fact is I slow her down. Jackie's not as smart as me and obviously I'm not as agile as her, but that doesn't make any difference. I help her with her homework and we go to the mall together. Can I ask you another question?

MICHAEL:

Last one... then it's your turn.

He hands her the book.

HALLEY:
Were you badly wounded?

MICHAEL:
Displaced comminuted fractures on the tibia and the fibula, and a couple compound fractures.

HALLEY:
That sounds bad.

MICHAEL:
Rehab's intense but I'm trying for my BFT soon as I get clearance.

HALLEY:
What's a BFT?

MICHAEL:
Battle Fitness Test. You have to do stuff like march thirteen kilometres carrying sixty pounds of gear—even if your job's just sitting at a desk you have to be a soldier first or you're out—but me, I'm not out—I'm going back to Petawawa.

HALLEY:
(coughs) The name Petawawa comes from the Algonquin word *biidaawewe*, which means "where one hears a noise like this"? *(coughs)* My grandmother told me that. She used to work at an Esso station in Deep River.

MICHAEL:
Can I ask you a question?

HALLEY:
Sure.

MICHAEL:
What happened that you can't walk?

HALLEY:
(takes a moment) Three years ago I had a very very very very bad skiing accident. It was a cold windy day and all the parents came to watch. While the coach was setting up the course on the beginners' hill—I started getting cold... but instead of going back into the chalet I decided to warm up by skiing down the intermediate hill. So... anyway, when I got to the top I looked down and saw that the wind had blown most of the new snow off and the hill was icy and sparkling and I thought it would be good practise for the race ahead so I pushed off and suddenly I was speeding down the hill going faster and faster and faster and I could hear my heart beating in my ears and I loved the feeling of lifting off like a huge airplane flying up, up into the clouds... and I woke up in the emergency ward.

MICHAEL:
That's lousy luck.

HALLEY:
The accident ended my Olympic career. I had the perfect build for a ski racer—a bit of weight for strength, not too tall, plus I possess steely determination and fearlessness—that's what my coach said. But I try not to look back. I look ahead. Do you?

MICHAEL:
What?

HALLEY:
Look ahead?

MICHAEL:
Let's keep reading.

HALLEY:
Okay.

(*reads*) "After complicated journeyings"—that's not a word; at least not a modern word—"After complicated journeyings with many pauses, there had come months of monotonous life in a camp... He had grown to regard himself merely as a part of a vast blue demonstration."

He uses a lot of descriptive words and colours, doesn't he?

MICHAEL:
...yeah.

HALLEY:
Mrs. Parker told us it's like he was painting the story.

She hands MICHAEL *the book.*

MICHAEL:
(*reads*) "From the stories, the youth imagined the red, live bones sticking out through slits in the faded uniforms. Still, he could not put a whole faith in veterans' tales, for recruits were their prey... However, he perceived now that it did not greatly matter what kind of soldiers he was going to fight, so long as they fought, which fact no one disputed. There was a more serious problem. He lay in his bunk pondering upon it. He tried to mathematically prove to himself that he would not run from a battle."

Does he get killed?

HALLEY:
Who—Henry?

MICHAEL:
Is that this guy's name?

HALLEY:
Yes. Henry Fleming.

MICHAEL:
Does he get killed?

HALLEY:
Spoiler alert. Not telling.

MICHAEL closes the book and hands it back to her.

MICHAEL:
I'm not reading anymore unless you tell me.

HALLEY:
...okay, he gets hurt. It's not really a war wound but he pretends it is so he can prove he didn't run, that he stood and fought, at least that's what Mrs. Parker said and I believe her because she reads lots of books. We have in-depth conversations during recess and after school. She's always recommending books to me. Do you know what she did last fall?

MICHAEL:
What?

HALLEY:
She asked *me* to suggest books that she might order for the school library. I might be a librarian when I grow up or maybe a forensic detective like Edmond Locard. Do you know who he is?

MICHAEL:
No.

HALLEY:
He's French, from France—he started the idea of forensic science: *Every contact leaves a trace.*

MICHAEL:
Does Henry die at the end?

HALLEY:

No. *(starts to cough)* ...he doesn't.

HALLEY continues to cough and cough.

MICHAEL:

Want a drink?

HALLEY:

I better go. *(coughs and coughs)* I have to be in the lobby when the mobility bus arrives. They don't like to wait around.

MICHAEL:

There's a Pepsi machine down at the end of the hall. I've got change somewhere.

HALLEY:

(coughs) No thanks.

MICHAEL:

Sure you don't want one to take with you?

HALLEY:

No, too cold outside. *(coughs)* See you next week.

MICHAEL:

Could I borrow that book?

HALLEY:

It belongs to the school library.

MICHAEL:

I'll take good care of it.

HALLEY:

I think you just want to read ahead to find out what happens.

MICHAEL:
I'll only read the next chapter.

She hands him the book and keeps coughing.

Thanks.

HALLEY:
Bye...

Exit HALLEY.

MICHAEL *sits on the bed and opens the book... finds his place...*

MICHAEL:
(reads) "A little panic-fear grew in his mind. As his imagination went forward to a fight, he saw hideous possibilities. He contemplated the lurking menaces of the future, and failed in an effort to see himself standing stoutly in the midst of them."

(looks up from the book) Are you listening?

"He sprang from the bunk and began to pace nervously to and fro. 'Good Lord, what's th' matter with me?' he said aloud. He felt that in this crisis his laws of life were useless."

He holds the book... and closes his eyes tight.

SCENE THREE

One week later.

The dusky rays of the late afternoon sun shine through the side window.

MICHAEL, *who has put some effort into his appearance, clutches* The Red Badge of Courage *in one hand and paces.*

Enter HALLEY, *her pack on her lap.*

HALLEY:
The snow's crunchy today.

MICHAEL:
Hi.

HALLEY:
Do you get to go outside much?

MICHAEL:
I go out to smoke.

HALLEY:
Smoking is bad for—

MICHAEL:
You're *way* too young to lecture me.

HALLEY:
Sorry.

She pulls off her hat and mitts, opens her parka. She's wearing her uniform.

MICHAEL:
(to the point) I really like this book, eh. I like how the story follows Henry—how it's about what he saw and what he felt about it.

HALLEY:
Great. Let's jump straight to the juicy parts in Chapter Five, to the big battle scene.

MICHAEL:
(to the point) I finished it.

HALLEY:
Chapter Five?

MICHAEL:
Whole thing.

HALLEY:
You finished the whole book?

MICHAEL:
Yeah.

HALLEY:
I figured you would—I even planned to bring more books today but I just heard the worst worst worst news possible.

MICHAEL:
...what?

HALLEY:
Jackie, my so-called best friend, she didn't tell me this in person but Mince—Mince is a friend of Jackie's and sometimes she talks to me—anyway, this afternoon Mince came into the library and I overheard her telling Mrs. Parker

that Jackie's mother might get a job in Calgary—which is 3,336 and one half kilometres from here!

MICHAEL:
Is that good, I guess… no, not good?

HALLEY:
No not good. Jackie lives with her mom and that means she'll have to move to Calgary too, or maybe she'd stay with her dad until school finishes in June then move. It actually doesn't matter when she moves, the point is—the upsetting horrible point is that Jackie might be leaving.

MICHAEL:
That's a rough deal.

HALLEY:
…I wish we were talking—I mean, we'll be talking again. We always make up. She's my only real friend. No one likes to admit they only have one real friend—everyone brags that they have a million friends but—I mean I have friends in Pathfinders and friends I hang out with in the library, but I only have one friend who actually cares about me.

Silence.

MICHAEL:
You want a Pepsi?

HALLEY:
No thanks.

MICHAEL:
A bag of chips? They got Barbecue, Dill Pickle…

HALLEY:
No thanks.

MICHAEL:
They got chocolate bars, too.

HALLEY:
I wish we had something to read.

MICHAEL:
We could read some of this.

HALLEY:
You've read it and I've read it—it's no fun now.

MICHAEL:
...maybe we could read our favourite parts again.

HALLEY:
...okay.

MICHAEL:
You start.

He hands her the book.

HALLEY:
I like the part where Henry runs into the forest then he sees a squirrel that—

She opens the book, which has many pages folded over.

OH MY GOD!

MICHAEL:
What?

HALLEY:
You folded pages over!

MICHAEL:
Sorry.

HALLEY:
(trying to flatten the pages out) Mrs. Parker gets apoplectic when people fold pages over—it's a no-no!

MICHAEL *tries to help flatten the pages but it's not a job for two people.*

MICHAEL:
Sorry...

HALLEY:
...it's somewhere around here...

(reads) "Presently he began to feel the effects of the war atmosphere—a blistering sweat, a sensation that his eyeballs were about to crack like hot stones. A burning roar filled his ears. Following this came a red rage."

See, the colour red again—"red rage."

MICHAEL:
Yeah.

HALLEY:
(reads) "He fought frantically for respite for his senses, for air, as a babe being smothered attacks the deadly blankets."

Do you now what Mrs. Parker would call that?

MICHAEL:
What?

HALLEY:
A simile.

MICHAEL:
Yeah well I don't blame her but...

He takes the book and quickly finds the place she was looking for.

...the part you're looking for is on... page forty-two.

He hands the book back to her.

HALLEY:
How many times did you read this?

MICHAEL:
Just twice.

She glances at him—perhaps he's read it more than twice.

HALLEY:
(reads) "After a time the sound of musketry grew faint... The sun, suddenly apparent, blazed among the trees... A bird flew on lighthearted wing. Off was the rumble of death. It seemed now that Nature had no ears. This landscape gave him assurance... It was the religion of peace—"

MICHAEL:
But later he turned against those thoughts—

HALLEY:
Let me finish—

(reads) "He threw a pine cone at a jovial squirrel, and he ran with chattering fear... The youth felt triumphant at this exhibition. There was the law, he said. Nature had given him a sign. The squirrel, immediately upon recognizing danger, had taken to his legs without ado."

I like that Henry believed he was right to save his own life by running, just like the squirrel ran from the flying pine cone.

MICHAEL:

He thought he was right until he stumbled upon that dead soldier—then everything changed, eh. Death scared him so much he ran back and joined a column of wounded soldiers, then he met Jim, who was *actually* dying. That dead body Henry saw in the woods? That was him seeing the future.

HALLEY:

It's called foreshadowing.

MICHAEL:

Whatever—the point is when he stumbled into that body he stumbled into the future and into Jim's death and even into his own.

HALLEY:

Henry doesn't die.

MICHAEL:

I know, but death is always your battle, eh. Even when you're not fighting, even when you're just watching TV, you battle death—the death of your buddies, of yourself, your dreams, the kind of person you thought you were or the kind of person you are. War is about how you face death. Look at Jim Conklin, eh, and how he faced his—reaching out to Henry, and poor Henry not knowing what the hell to do...

He takes the book from HALLEY, *unfolds the corner of a page, and starts reading.*

"He yelled in horror. Tottering forward he laid a quivering hand upon the man's arm. As the latter slowly turned his waxlike features toward him the youth screamed: 'Gawd! Jim Conklin!' "

You read Henry.

He moves closer to her so they can share the book.

HALLEY:

(*as Henry*) "Gawd! Jim Conklin!"

MICHAEL:
(as Jim) " 'Hello, Henry.' "

HALLEY:
" 'Oh, Jim—oh, Jim—oh, Jim—' "

MICHAEL:
" 'Where yeh been, Henry? I thought mebbe yeh got keeled over. There's been thunder t' pay t'-day... I was out there... An', Lord, what a circus! An', b'jiminey, I got shot—I got shot. Yes, b'jiminey, I got shot.' "

HALLEY:
" 'I'll take care of yeh, Jim! I'll take care of yeh! I swear t' Gawd I will!' "

MICHAEL:
" 'I was allus a good friend t' yeh, wa'n't I, Henry? I've allus been a pretty good feller, ain't I?' "

HALLEY:
"The youth had reached an anguish where the sobs scorched him. He strove to express his loyalty... However, the tall soldier seemed suddenly to forget all those fears... He went stonily forward. The youth wished his friend to lean upon him, but the other always shook his head and strangely protested."

MICHAEL:
" 'No—no—no—leave me be—leave me be'... His tall figure stretched itself to its full height... Then it began to swing forward, slow and straight, in the manner of a falling tree. A swift muscular contortion made the left shoulder strike the ground first. The body seemed to bounce a little way from the earth."

HALLEY:
"The youth had watched, spellbound... His face had been twisted into an expression of every agony he had imagined for his friend. He... gazed upon the pastelike face. The mouth was open and—"

MICHAEL:
Okay, that's enough.

She takes the book and closes it.

HALLEY:
It's so sad. Sad times a thousand.

Silence.

Can I ask you a question?

MICHAEL:
What?

HALLEY:
Are we going to win the war?

MICHAEL:
It's not just us—it's a NATO-led coalition.

HALLEY:
Are they going to win?

MICHAEL:
No one's gonna win.

HALLEY:
Why not?

MICHAEL:
Lot of reasons… mostly because it's a counter-insurgency.

HALLEY:
What's that mean?

MICHAEL:

We're tasked with helping the government of Afghanistan serve the needs of their people by separating insurgents from the local populations—except you can't defeat an insurgency, best you can do is marginalize it.

HALLEY:

Does that mean we're not going to win?

MICHAEL:

There never was going to be a victory.

HALLEY:

But Ms. Wren said that girls over there can go to school now. That's a kind of victory, isn't it?

MICHAEL:

Some of them get acid thrown in their face on the way to school—and there's schools we haven't finished building and never will. Why should the Afghan people believe we're there to help them? They know what foreign occupation means so why the hell should they trust us, eh? We ask them the same stupid questions they've been asked for years. Do your crops get better? No. Do your living conditions improve? Hardly. Education helps but I've seen some real ugly shit.

HALLEY:

My stepfather says war is obscene.

MICHAEL:

He's right.

HALLEY's cellphone rings.

HALLEY:

Let's just stop having wars, okay?

MICHAEL:
Won't get any argument from me there.

HALLEY:
(into her phone) I'll be right there. *(to MICHAEL)* Bus is here—I have to go. I'll return this to the library and bring in new ones next week.

MICHAEL:
Can I keep it a bit longer?

HALLEY:
You already read it twice.

MICHAEL:
It's a really good book.

HALLEY:
Okay...

She hands the book back to him.

...just don't fold over any more pages.

MICHAEL:
I'll flatten these ones out.

HALLEY:
It was fun reading with you today.

MICHAEL:
Yeah, it was.

HALLEY:
See you next week.

MICHAEL:
Yeah, for sure.

Exit HALLEY.

He takes his laptop and starts banging on the keyboard.

"The night was sprinkled with stars... the... the black sky made Mark... Martin... Mitchell... no, Aidan—the black sky made Aidan and..." What name do you want? Devon? Danny? You like Danny? ...okay. "...black sky made Aidan and Danny feel like they were caught up in some vast demonstration, that tonight was going to be more than just another cold night of endless reconnaissance in blackout conditions in the endless—long friggin', endless friggin' sentence—because something's gonna happen..."

He continues banging on the keyboard.

SCENE FOUR

One week later. Light comes through the side window—the days are getting longer now. It is grey outside, raining.

MICHAEL clasps a few printed pages in his hand. Impatient, he opens the door and looks down the corridor then comes back into the room. He goes over to the window and looks out.

Enter HALLEY, no hat, no mitts, and her parka already open, uniform on underneath. She's wearing purple rubber boots instead of winter boots.

HALLEY:
Guess what?

MICHAEL:
What?

HALLEY:
You have to guess.

MICHAEL:
You read ten books in two hours.

HALLEY:
No—last Friday, when I was getting things out of my locker, Jackie came up to me and said, "I miss you." Isn't that incredible?

MICHAEL:
Yeah, I guess so.

HALLEY:
We spent Saturday at her house so I could help her with her math project then we went to see *Bridge to Terabithia*. She told me her mom's flying to Calgary this week for an interview but that she doesn't really want the job.

MICHAEL:
That's good, yes?

HALLEY:
Yes, that's very good. Here...

She pulls two books from her packsack.

Which one do you want to read—*All Quiet on the Western Front* or *The Iliad*?

MICHAEL:
Do you think... could we read this instead?

HALLEY:
What is it?

MICHAEL:
A story.

He hands her his printed pages. She takes them.

HALLEY:
(reads) Armstrong's War.

Who wrote it?

MICHAEL:
I did.

HALLEY:
You wrote a story... wow.

MICHAEL:

It's just… nothing. Just a story.

HALLEY:

We can take turns reading it out loud.

MICHAEL:

Some of the language is rough, eh—swearing and stuff.

HALLEY:

Mrs. Parker says that anyone can pepper their writing with swear words but it takes a good writer to make those words sound necessary.

MICHAEL:

…I don't think I'm that person…

HALLEY:

(reads) "My name is Michael Armstrong. I'm a Canadian soldier and this is a story about my friends Aidan and Danny. The night sky was sprinkled with stars. It hung like a black sparkling tarp over Aidan as he walked quietly along a dusty road. The road had become a sorrowful blackness and he could barely see in front of him then Aidan heard a weak groan. The sound was so unexpected his gut dropped to his boots. Where was it coming from? Maybe it was some fuck lying low on the other side of the *wadi*"—what's a *wadi*?

MICHAEL:

Dried-up riverbed.

HALLEY:

"…on the other side of the *wadi* or maybe it was just the maw of a donkey. Maybe it was coming from Danny who was up ahead about seventy-five metres, except Danny never made noise and he had eyes on the back of his head. Drop Danny in the middle of nowhere 125 kilometres north of Kandahar at 0300 hours and you have the perfect marriage between soldier and task. Aidan flipped on his night goggles and the world turns puke green.

He listened harder but heard nothing. Maybe it had just been the sound of swallows flying overhead.

"Earlier that night Intel had come into their base that enemy movement had been sighted on the road that was going to be used for a village medical out-reach so Aidan and Danny were on recon to make sure the road and building were clear. It was below zero and Aidan kept looking up at the white stars."

MICHAEL *reaches for the pages.*

MICHAEL:
My turn.

"Yesterday he and Danny were in a trance of astonishment when they saw the bluish white Hindu Kush Mountains in the distance. When they first met they'd talk about taking an Alexander the Great walking tour from Greece to Afghanistan but these days Danny was more interested in the future than the past. He was getting married on his next leave and Aidan would be Best Man. Danny's fiancée, Trish, and Danny's mother were in charge of planning—purple ties, black suits, a burgundy theme for the reception, five different colours of flowers, and a thousand other decisions more complicated than any battle plan Aidan ever trained for."

HALLEY *takes the pages as her cellphone rings.*

HALLEY:
"There was that sound again, like a moan, but he couldn't see anything—"

Sorry, it's... *(into the phone)* I'm BUSY READING... yeah, the soldier... Mom, I'm fine, I'm not hardly coughing, I'm fine fine fine. Bye. *(to MICHAEL)* Sorry.

"But he couldn't see anything. The enemy were ghosts. Sometimes the only shape they took was in what they left behind—empty water bottles and prayer mats and red blood trails. When they actually took shape they were ordinary figures standing in the distance. He knew a lot of them were poor and angry, and even though he was afraid of them he tried to keep them human at least in his mind but he couldn't protect himself from getting pissed off as more soldiers were being killed by IEDs." *(to* MICHAEL*)* What's IEDs?

MICHAEL:
Improvised explosive devices.

HALLEY:
"Aidan walked faster. He imagined people secure in his eagle-eyed prowess but he also longed for the sky to usher in the colours of dawn when KABOOM… the world lifted up in front of Aidan like a red spitting volcano."

Do you want to read?

He takes back the pages.

MICHAEL:
"The blast wave knocked him over but it was someone screaming that got him back up on his feet again. Punching through a cloud of dust he started to run, a red panic growing in his mind. Most soldiers carry talismans but Aidan had left his tiny white seashell behind when the order came to head out. Now it didn't matter anymore if he believed in anything or not—he just automatically started praying, "Please take my legs, my arms, but don't take my friend.""

He hands her the pages.

Here.

HALLEY:
"They had trained together at Petawawa and Wainwright or Wainwrightistan as it was called—a mock Afghan village outside Edmonton—and when they got to Kandahar Province they leaguered up along half a dozen *wadis* sleeping under the sky beside a LAV with hardly a bug tent…" What's a L—

MICHAEL:
Light-armoured vehicle.

HALLEY:
"...hardly a bug tent to crawl under, cutting through boredom by arguing about the Senators versus the Leafs. Sometimes they organized wrestling matches between camel spiders, giving them names like Piss Giant and Lucky Legs then watching the creatures get tangled up in each other. The heat made Aidan feel that his eyeballs would crack but every night the stars made him forget the heat and the fear of not knowing what's going to happen. Twice he'd been behind LAVs that got hit by IEDs and he had to help peel body parts off the inside of red smouldering wrecks,"—yuck—"fellow soldiers of astonishing valour who got lost in terrible destruction. Death was always in front of Aidan and here it was calling him again so he ran faster, his pants full, 'Mother bitch, no,' he screamed when he saw Danny lying on his back covered in chunks of dark gold sand. No helmet, flak jacket torn open—"

MICHAEL:
But you're not ready, eh.

HALLEY:
Pardon?

MICHAEL:
...you're never prepared for that.

HALLEY:
Should I stop reading?

MICHAEL:
...just for a second.

She gives him a Kleenex even though he is not crying.

HALLEY:

Just in case. I've got lots more. I even have a miniature first-aid kit. My mom outfits me as if I'm going to find myself in some calamity on my way to school. She makes me carry baby wipes and emergency food and a flashlight—baby wipes are for babies...

Silence.

Do you want me to get you a Pepsi or a bag of chips?

MICHAEL:

No. I'm fine now.

HALLEY:

I can call a nurse.

MICHAEL:

I'm fine.

HALLEY:

There should be a button by your bed.

MICHAEL:

Don't bother—no one comes anyway.

HALLEY:

No one?

MICHAEL:

They stick their head through the door at 0700 to make sure you haven't run away or done yourself in, then you never see them again.

HALLEY:

Are you sure you're all right?

MICHAEL:
I'm just sad, okay?

HALLEY:
Okay.

MICHAEL:
Sadness is a very normal very ordinary emotion.

HALLEY:
I know.

MICHAEL:
Keep reading.

HALLEY:
"Somebody knew they were coming. Someone had been watching and signalled somebody else with a fucking cellphone or fucking fake donkey call... then Aidan heard the crackle of RPG fire in—"

MICHAEL:
Rocket-propelled grenade.

HALLEY:
"...RPG fire in the distance. He put his hands under Danny's armpits so he could haul him closer to the *wadi* for safety... that's when he noticed pink and red chunks and burnt skin hanging in slabs from what would have been the lower part of Danny's belly..."

She stops reading.

This is hard to read.

MICHAEL *takes the pages from her.*

MICHAEL:

"Aidan started puking orange brown crap then he knelt down beside Danny to see if he was still breathing. He was gurgling silent puffs and whispering, *'Killlll me... killlll me...'* Aidan remembered the blood promise they'd made early in their tour—something that only each other would ever know about. 'Promise to do this for me.' 'Yes, you have my word.' Aidan saw that Danny's eyes were open and staring into a great distance as he headed down towards the banks of the River Styx, the mythic boundary between Earth and the Underworld that they'd read about in a book about Greek warriors. Danny had turned to blood. First you're flesh and blood then you're just blood. With one hand Aidan squeezed Danny's nostrils together and with the other he covered Danny's mouth. War is not clean—sometimes you have to make it clean.

"He stayed kneeling beside Danny until backup arrived. When the medic removed Danny's dog tag Aidan suddenly remembered his own grandfather telling him how he pulled a dead buddy out of a sinkhole in France.

"By 0400 the sky was covered in pink and orange and red streaks, and by sundown Aidan was one of the honour guards carrying Danny's coffin towards the belly of a plane. The coffin was full of ice.

"He accompanied it to Trenton and met Danny's family and Trish, a young woman with red swollen eyes. He told Danny's mother that her son was fearless because he ran towards everything and that his MSN was *diegoingforward*, but she was not listening, she was in shock.

"Later Aidan would lie in bed wondering what the swallows saw when they looked down and watched him leaning over his friend.

"For the rest of Aidan's life Danny would walk into his dreams, fit and happy. He'd never lose his 'Go Leafs Go' bravado, and they would still talk about taking that Alexander the Great tour someday."

The end.

Sorry about some of the language and graphic stuff.

Silence.

HALLEY:
...wow.

MICHAEL:
When I was writing this I started to remember the colours of Afghanistan, the mountains, all the different shades of sand and sky.

HALLEY:
...that really scrambled my brain.

MICHAEL:
Sometimes being a soldier has no colour—other times it's just all colour.

HALLEY:
It's written really well... but I don't know; I don't know it's... it's kind of stupid.

MICHAEL:
...stupid?

HALLEY:
...not stupid but...

MICHAEL:
I probably used too many colours too many times, especially red.

HALLEY:
No, it's not the colours it's... I don't understand why Aidan killed his friend.

MICHAEL:
They made a pact.

HALLEY:
To kill his friend?

MICHAEL:
It was a mutual promise.

HALLEY:
How can you make a promise that ends in someone dying?

MICHAEL:
That's not why he gave him the *coup de grâce*.

HALLEY:
The what?

MICHAEL:
Mercy stroke—to end the suffering of a mortally wounded soldier.

HALLEY:
Oh.

MICHAEL:
That was their pact, eh—they promised each other that if one of them got so badly wounded they'd be unable to live like a man then the other one would administer mercy.

HALLEY:
But… but what if Danny was laying there and he couldn't talk and couldn't move but inside his head he's screaming, *"I changed my mind I changed my mind—please don't kill me."*

MICHAEL:
It would have been wrong if they hadn't discussed it ahead of time and if Aidan had just taken matters into his own hands, but they talked about it many times.

HALLEY:

But how did Aidan know his friend wouldn't get better—maybe not better, but how did he know that his friend wouldn't just live somehow?

MICHAEL:

Like I said, they discussed it and decided that neither one wanted to just "live somehow."

HALLEY:

That doesn't make sense. How could Aidan make a decision like that in two seconds?

MICHAEL:

It was longer than two seconds.

HALLEY:

Okay, ten seconds.

MICHAEL:

It was more than a minute—and look at all the thoughts and feelings that went through his head. All their training together and—

HALLEY:

How did he know Danny's life wasn't going to be a life—he's not a doctor—even a doctor wouldn't know!

MICHAEL:

Half of Danny was missing.

HALLEY:

Then he should have searched for Danny's legs instead of just going through crap in his own head.

MICHAEL:

It's not crap—he was assessing his—

HALLEY:
Where were his legs?

MICHAEL:
He saw that Danny had no chance.

HALLEY:
How do you know he had no chance?

MICHAEL:
Because that's what Aidan told me.

HALLEY:
You should call it *Aidan's War* instead of *Armstrong's War*—and you should make him way less selfish. He's so eager to keep his stupid mercy promise that he didn't even look for his friend's legs. Mrs. Parker would call that sloppy story writing and it makes Aidan look completely dishonourable—you don't kill someone just because they lose their legs.

MICHAEL:
That's not why Aidan killed him.

HALLEY:
Then why did he kill him?

MICHAEL:
Aidan saw with his own eyes that if Danny lived he'd end up living the kind of life that he told Aidan he absolutely did not want to live!

HALLEY:
No one can see the future—not even fortune tellers!

MICHAEL:
Those two trained together and deployed together. They came to understand they could count on each other and they both saw what happens when an IED detonates under a buddy—that's part one. Then when you're on leave

and visit your severely injured buddy you see part two. I'm not talking about guys who've lost a limb or two or even a triple amputee—I'm talking about when the damage is so catastrophic that the guy has to live in an acute-care situation for the rest of his life with ten medical personnel looking after him 24-7 and his mother or his wife basically living in the next room. Sure, he might have been a fine soldier, and could have been a great husband and a wonderful father—but in that situation he's no longer a man.

HALLEY:
But he's alive—that's all that counts!

MICHAEL:
He's alive, sure—it's a medical miracle, and thank god for miracles, but sometimes guys don't wanna be a medical miracle. Danny had nothing left—not even his junk.

HALLEY:
What junk?

MICHAEL:
His… a man's reproductive equipment.

HALLEY:
You mean penis and stuff.

MICHAEL:
…yeah. That's just the way guys are.

HALLEY:
What way?

MICHAEL:
…no one wants to live if they don't have a reason to. Guys want to have a relationship. They want to be able to love somebody. Look, it's hard talking about this with you because you have your own problems—

HALLEY:
Don't start feeling sorry for me.

MICHAEL:
I don't—I'm just trying to explain things from a soldier's—a male soldier's point of view, eh. These two guys I wrote about decided that if either one of them was severely wounded they didn't want to keep living if there was no possibility of living a full life. Even if his legs had been found there was no place to put them—Robbie was a mess—no bone structure left, no torso!

HALLEY:
Robbie?

MICHAEL:
I mean Danny.

Silence.

HALLEY:
I think your two friends were totally weird and dishonourable. If Mrs. Parker read this story she'd probably say the same—

MICHAEL:
Don't you go telling her about my story!

HALLEY:
I'm not planning to, but if I were you I'd rewrite it and have Danny—

MICHAEL:
What do you know—you've never been in a battle.

HALLEY:
Okay, I don't know anything about war—I mean I'm twelve. I don't feel twelve when I'm reading but I feel twelve when I'm... *not* reading.

MICHAEL:

Halley, I never talked about this kind of thing before... never put anything down on paper, that's for sure.

HALLEY:

It's obvious you were inspired by *The Red Badge of Courage* and maybe stuff like soldiers killing their soldier friends happened in the Civil War but Stephen Crane didn't write about it because he knew if he did people probably wouldn't read his book.

MICHAEL:

He didn't write about them because he never went to war.

HALLEY:

He did too!

MICHAEL:

No he did not!

HALLEY:

He did too!

MICHAEL:

I looked him up. When his book came out people just figured he was in the war but he wasn't born until after the friggin' war was over!

HALLEY:

Are you sure?

MICHAEL:

Go ahead—check if you don't believe me. They think he used notes from the Battle of Chancellorsville to help write his book.

HALLEY:

...it's hard to believe he didn't go to war.

MICHAEL:

He didn't go to war!

HALLEY:

Okay—he didn't go... but it doesn't matter because he *imagined* how war felt—that's what your imagination is for—to imagine how something *feels*!

MICHAEL:

I don't have to imagine—I actually went to war, and maybe my two friends are not honourable soldiers in your eyes or in the military's eyes or in Mrs. Parker's eyes or in their mothers' eyes but they are honourable in my eyes! Aidan kept his word and that takes courage because finally that's all you have—*your* word. What I promise I will do, I will do and you can stake your life on it, and that is honourable.

HALLEY:

If I were you I'd be ashamed of your friends. That's probably why you're always hiding under the bed—you're ashamed of what you know.

MICHAEL:

Who the fuck do you think you are barging in here like a tank—barging in like those other do-gooders—who the fuck are you anyway? Take away your books and your Girl Guide shit and you're just a lonely girl with no friends— oh, sorry—you got one friend—a lonely girl with *one* friend who likes to rub up against people you think are more helpless than you are so that you can feel better about your lonely, friendless, CUMBERSOME SELF!

HALLEY:

Fuck you.

MICHAEL:

Fuck you, too.

HALLEY:

Fuck you times a thousand!

Exit HALLEY. MICHAEL *sticks his head out the door.*

MICHAEL:
Hey...

Exit MICHAEL.

(off) ...you forgot your stupid book...

Enter MICHAEL.

...your red green purple shit-brown blue damned friggin' book.

He rips apart The Red Badge of Courage.

Robbie, you asshole—see what you've done, eh? It's your fault... Robbie...?

MICHAEL *begins to realize that something has changed. He looks around... feeling lost.*

...Robbie...? Robbie...?

He listens to the silence.

SCENE FIVE

One week later. Light comes in through the side window.

MICHAEL holds a bouquet of red flowers wrapped in plastic as he looks out the window.

He waits and waits… then he tosses the flowers into the trash can and gets down and does five lopsided push-ups.

Enter HALLEY—parka open, uniform on, no hat or mitts, wearing running shoes.

MICHAEL:
Figured you weren't coming back.

HALLEY:
I was in the lobby for twenty minutes, but I need that badge and I'm going to get it if it's the last thing I do because I'm a Pathfinder and even though you think it's just silly Girl Guide shit—

MICHAEL:
I apologize for—

HALLEY:
I'm not finished! The name Pathfinder was taken from the writings of Lord Baden-Powell, the founder of Guiding and Scouting, who decided that a special name would be given to people who were good at finding their way in a strange country and you're a strange country to me… plus I need that book back—it's a week overdue.

MICHAEL tries to fish the flowers out of the garbage as nonchalantly as possible then presents them to her.

MICHAEL:
I apologize for insulting you and for swearing, here…

She looks suspiciously at the flowers and does not take them.

HALLEY:
How come they were in the garbage?

MICHAEL:
I put them there two seconds ago because I thought you weren't coming.

HALLEY:
I'm not very interested in flowers.

He's not sure what to do with the flowers.

The bus will be back soon and I can't be one second late because Jackie's coming to our house tonight for spaghetti and meatballs then I'm helping her with her science project then she's sleeping over because her mom's in Calgary. She got a job offer but hasn't said yes or no—anyway, we have to hurry…

She digs in her pack, pulls out two printed pages, and hands them to him.

…it's short.

MICHAEL:
What is it?

HALLEY:
Something I wrote last night in a very big rush.

MICHAEL:
Armstrong's War. That's the same title as mine.

HALLEY:
Yes, but it's a completely different story.

MICHAEL:

"Lucy earned all her Brownie badges by the time she was eight. In one month alone she earned Swimming, Bicycling, Hiking, Water Safety, Mountain Climbing, and Woodwork. She advanced to Guides on her ninth birthday and earned badges for Endangered Species, Outdoor Adventure, Bird Watching, and Ecology. After her skiing accident, Lucy's grandmother came to live with them. One day in class, Brittany MacDonald-Lapinski called Lucy a 'Fatso on Wheels,' so Lucy called her a *nose-sucking, snot-mouthed, manure-lipped hippo*. Lucy was sent home and her grandmother said, "Next time someone insults you, you invoke the Armstrong clan motto: *Invictus Maneo: I remain unvanquished*. Her grandmother said it would be both a shield and a sword."

Your turn.

HALLEY:

"Lucy completed the Girl Guide requirements and became a Pathfinder. Then as part of acquiring her Community Service badge, Lucy met a Canadian soldier named Aidan who was being rehabilitated. Aidan told Lucy about his time in Afghanistan. One night Aidan and his best friend Danny were walking along a blacked-out road looking for enemy insurgencies. Aidan was admiring the beautiful stars overhead and Danny was thinking about Trish, his fiancée, who was studying Library Sciences back home in Canada. Trish was busy picking out her wedding dress and planning the wedding dinner menu. Her dress would be Organza with a Sweetheart Neckline and a Ball Gown Skirt and a Train. The dinner would be four courses—appetizers, Turkey Dill Mouse and Mushroom Caps—"

MICHAEL:

Sure that's Dill Mouse, not Dill something else?

HALLEY:

It's spelled M.O.U.S.E. Maybe it's supposed to be shaped like a mouse—anyway...

"...then an entrée, Tomato Cucumber Salad, then the main course would be Herb-Crusted Sirloin Beef with Seasonal Vegetables OR Chicken Breasts with Honey Mustard or BBQ Sauce with your choice of Potato or Rice and a five-storey Wedding Cake covered in purple and pink candy flowers. Meanwhile, back in the war, Aidan heard a strange sound and grew afraid."

Your turn…

MICHAEL:
"It sounded like a donkey mooing—"

HALLEY:
Oops, that should be moaning.

MICHAEL:
"…like a donkey moaning. He listened but couldn't see any enemies through his night goggles, only Danny who was walking up ahead. Suddenly everything went KA-BOOM and his world turned red. When they had received the call earlier saying there were enemies on the road and that they had to go check it out, Aidan grabbed his white seashell and stuffed it into his camouflaged pocket… now he was running with all his might towards his fallen comrade, cursing and praying at the same time. 'Danny,' he screamed when he saw his friend lying on the ground half covered in sand. He lifted Danny to a safe place and that's when he saw that Danny's—"

HALLEY's cellphone rings.

HALLEY:
(into the phone) Yeah—be there in a minute. *(to MICHAEL)* Sorry, keep reading.

MICHAEL:
"…he saw that Danny's legs were missing so he laid his friend back down and checked his breathing. Danny begged Aidan to end his life but Aidan called a rescue helicopter, then he looked for Danny's legs and found them lying together. When the helicopter landed Aidan gave the legs to a medic to put on ice, then he helped the medic lift his wounded friend off the battlefield."

I think I know where this story's going.

HALLEY:

No, you don't.

MICHAEL:

Did you stick on a happy ending?

She reaches over and takes the two pages from him.

HALLEY:

"They flew back to Canada. Sadly, Danny's legs could not be saved. He endured many surgeries so that someday he could be fitted with robotic legs. They already have myoelectric arms and bionic feet so robotic legs are only a few years away. Danny and Trish were married. Trish added two more dishes to the wedding menu—Trout baked in Puff Pastry and Chicken Breast Roll Ups with Asparagus. They hired a white Mobility Limousine decorated with pink Kleenex hearts. Danny wore a tuxedo and Aidan, his Best Man, wheeled him down the aisle. Trish quit Library Sciences to study medicine so she could be a doctor and look after her husband and have four children. Their family—"

MICHAEL:

That's not what really happened.

HALLEY:

I know what really happened.

MICHAEL:

No you don't!

HALLEY:

No fair—you got to read your story—let me finish mine.

MICHAEL:

It didn't end that way.

HALLEY:
This is *my* story and *my* story has a happy ending!

"Their family and friends raised money to build a house with an elevator you can activate by remote control. Aidan became a hero for saving Danny's life—they both became heroes—and every year they are invited to participate in Remembrance Day services. Lucy was so inspired by the soldier's inspiring story"—oops, I used inspire twice in the same sentence."

HALLEY's *cellphone rings again, and continues to ring.*

"...that she volunteered to fill Birthday Boxes for Food Banks and knit socks for soldiers overseas. She worked hard and became the youngest person ever to earn a Canada Cord and the next day her mom and stepfather bought her a puppy named Buttons."

The end.

I ran out of time so I just added stuff about volunteering—

(into the phone) I said I'll be there in a sec, just SHUT UP SHUT UP SHUT UP SHUT UP—

MICHAEL:
Hey, take it easy—

HALLEY:
This always happens—right in the middle of everything important, "Hurry the bus is here hurry the bus is coming the bus is leaving the damn bus bus bus bus"—Jackie's right I *am* cumbersome. I wish I could just get up and run whenever I felt like it—run along the beach with a dog and my arms flung out like this and I'm laughing and running and my dog's paws are lifting up off the sand and we're running and running—but I can't even get out of this stupid chair by myself!

MICHAEL:

For someone who can't run you stand pretty tall.

HALLEY:

Yeah, sure—you're just saying that to make me feel better.

MICHAEL:

It's your personal Guiding Law—you said so yourself, eh. Not many people can endure having their Olympic dreams destroyed.

HALLEY:

For your information I don't always follow the Guiding Laws, not even my own personal one.

MICHAEL:

You still stand tall in my view. Take the friggin' compliment.

HALLEY:

...for your information it wasn't a skiing accident, it was a stupid car accident.

MICHAEL:

...what happened?

HALLEY:

My sister Clara was in the musical *Annie* at school and Mom was there on the opening night because she had to help with costumes.

Our house is twenty kilometres from the school, so the plan was Dad would drive me there when he came home from work. I wore pink tights and a purple dress. We were driving along the small highway that leads to the big highway when my dad said, "That guy must think he's in the Grand Prix..."

You know how in your story you had swallows looking down?

MICHAEL:

Yeah.

HALLEY:
...well, if birds were looking down they would have seen two humans lying in a ditch and a car lying sideways behind a small person with pink legs and a large person in a suit. The large person was lying on his stomach with one arm stretched up over his head as if reaching out.

My dad was calling my name in a kind of crying voice, over and over. I tried to crawl to him... but couldn't move.

The guy who smashed into us was so drunk he couldn't even get out of his car to help. My dad died. I ended up with a spinal cord injury.

MICHAEL:
That's hard. I'm sorry.

HALLEY:
Don't feel sorry for me.

MICHAEL:
I don't.

HALLEY:
I know you don't, it's just... sometimes I feel sorry for myself because I didn't have a choice. In the skiing story I chose to go down the hill. I chose to go fast and faster and reach for something... exhilarating—and it was just me, not my dad—my dad's still alive in the skiing story.

MICHAEL:
I don't feel sorry for you, not for one second, but I'm sorry you lost your dad.

Silence.

HALLEY:
...can I change my mind about the flowers?

MICHAEL:
Sure.

He hands her the flowers.

HALLEY:
Are you still mad at me?

MICHAEL:
I wasn't really mad at you—mostly just mad at myself.

HALLEY:
They smell nice.

MICHAEL:
I chose red because of Stephen Crane's book.

HALLEY:
Oh—where is the book?

MICHAEL:
...yeah, okay, just a sec...

He sheepishly takes The Red Badge of Courage *from the night table drawer and hands it to her. Almost every page is taped together—the book cannot even close.*

Sorry about the taped up pages.

HALLEY:
...oh... my... God... Mrs. Parker's going to have a heart attack when she sees this—she'll never let me take out another library book and she'll kick me out of the Reading Circle and I won't be able to spend time in library at recess and if Ms. Wren ever finds out about this I'm a dead duck—

MICHAEL:
Okay, okay—here...

He reaches into his wallet, takes out a twenty-dollar bill, and hands it to her, but she does not take it.

Give this to Mrs. Parker so she can buy a new—

HALLEY:
No—taking money goes directly against the spirit of volunteering—

MICHAEL:
I'm not giving it to *you*—it's for her to replace the book—

HALLEY:
What the hell happened to it?

MICHAEL:
I got angry and ripped it up.

HALLEY:
Ripping up a book is not going to sit well with Mrs. Parker.

MICHAEL:
Just give her the money and tell her... tell her I'm sorry.

HALLEY:
She'll never believe that a soldier would damage this book—she'll think I'm exaggerating or covering up or something—

MICHAEL:
Just take the money.

Her cellphone rings again.

HALLEY:
Okay—but you keep the book. *(takes the money)* I'll think up a story to tell her.

She answers her phone.

Oh my God, the bus is leaving... I'LL GET LEFT IN THE PARKING LOT THEN I'LL BE LATE FOR JACKIE AND I CAN'T BE LATE I JUST CAN'T... I CAN'T BE ONE SECOND LATE...

Quickly she swivels her wheelchair around and heads out the door.

HOLD YOUR FRIGGING HORSES—I'M COMING I'M COMING!

Exit HALLEY.

MICHAEL *puts down the book and picks up her story.*

MICHAEL:
...happy endings and stupid endings and endings that never end.

He tosses her story on the bed.

SCENE SIX

One week later. Lights are off but sun streams in through the side window.

The bed is perfectly made.

Enter HALLEY. *No hat, no mitts, an open spring jacket over her uniform.*

HALLEY:
…hi. Hello?

She wheels up to the bed, parks, and tries to look under it.

Hello?

Enter MICHAEL. *He is wearing his dress uniform, sans hat, and carries two bags of chips and two cans of Pepsi.*

How come you're in uniform?

MICHAEL:
Felt like dressing up for our last session.

HALLEY:
You look nice.

MICHAEL:
(offers her a bag of chips) There's a Pepsi for each of us, too.

HALLEY:
(takes the snacks) Thanks.

MICHAEL:

I've got some good news.

HALLEY:

What?

MICHAEL:

I'm leaving in a few days—if the doc ever comes around to sign my discharge.
Gonna try for my BFT in a couple weeks.

HALLEY:

I've got some good news and some bad news. I told Mrs. Parker that our neigh-
bours' dog, who's a German shepherd-American bulldog cross named Muffin,
stole the book out of my backpack and chewed it up but she said no problem
because there's a fund for replacing books so here's your money back...

She hands him the twenty-dollar bill. He takes it.

...and Jackie's mom didn't take the job, which is good, but she bought Jackie
a cowboy hat from Calgary and when Jackie put it on I said it didn't suit the
shape of her head which she interpreted as me saying her head is misshapen
which is absolutely not what I meant—but she got angry so now we're not
talking. Anyway, *(opening her pack)* since this is our last day and there's not
enough time to read a novel, I brought poems by Wilfred Owen. He was a
famous war poet who—oh, I almost forgot. You need to sign this...

She pulls a form out of her packsack and hands it to him along with a pen.

...the next badges I'm going to get are Create a Garden, Adopt a Tree, and
Foster a Pet.

He signs and returns the form to her.

MICHAEL:

When you go back to Ms. Condor you don't have to tell her you read to a wounded soldier and saved him from his sadness. Maybe that's what you were supposed to do but you did something way more important.

HALLEY:

What did I do?

MICHAEL:

You asked me to write a story.

HALLEY:

I didn't *ask* you to write a story.

MICHAEL:

Okay, you inspired me.

HALLEY:

Stephen Crane inspired you.

MICHAEL:

Okay, but you were the one who brought his book to me—can we agree about that?

HALLEY:

Yeah but you decided to write that story all by yourself.

MICHAEL:

Okay, okay, but you brought me war books when most people wouldn't have even come back, or they would've come back with books on cooking or glass-blowing, but you came back with *The Red Badge of Courage* and reading it made me want to write a story. I want to thank you... but I also want you to know that the story isn't true.

HALLEY:
…it's not?

MICHAEL:
No. There was no Aidan and no Danny—just Robbie and me.

HALLEY:
I kind of figured that.

MICHAEL:
I wanted the story to be true but it's—I mean, the first part's true up to where Robbie wanted me to… well you know what he wanted—so I blocked his nose and put my hand over his mouth, but then something terrible happened.

HALLEY:
What?

MICHAEL:
I started to hope; I couldn't help it—I started hoping and hoping, then I radioed for a Medevac. The medics searched but couldn't find his legs—that made me crazy—leaving parts of him there. Both of us were flown to Landstuhl—I didn't even know I'd been hurt until the medics told me—then at the hospital I heard the doctors were going to fly Robbie back to Canada to die, so I asked a nurse to take me to his room and… his eyes were open.

HALLEY:
I bet he was glad to see you.

MICHAEL:
His eyes just stared at me, eh—that's when I knew I'd done an awful thing because he used to talk about how he heard stories about his great-grandfather coming back from WWI shaking and coughing from mustard gas. Robbie was afraid he'd end up like him and I used to say, "No friggin' way something like that could happen in 2006," but it did.

HALLEY:
…what happened?

MICHAEL:
The explosion blew off his legs, an arm, sliced off his junk, shattered his pelvis into fifty-six pieces, ruptured his lungs, damaged his brain—he bled so much his blood had to be replaced four times but he didn't die.

HALLEY:
…oh. Where is—is he here in the hospital?

MICHAEL:
No, he's in an acute-care facility. His mother stays in a room beside him.

HALLEY:
Is Trish there with him, too?

MICHAEL:
There's no Trish. I made her up.

HALLEY:
I liked her. I'd like to think of her reading to Robbie.

MICHAEL:
Nobody's reading to him—he's deaf.

HALLEY:
But maybe he can feel the vibrations of your voice even if he can't actually hear the—

MICHAEL:
Look, you got a story about flying through the clouds and now I got a story about keeping my word—they're good stories but your dad's still dead and Robbie's still alive and I still don't understand what it means that he has to lie there suffering. I mean, we're soldiers—sacrifice is our job—but I don't

know anymore what mercy is or what courage is; all I know is that if it had been the other way round Robbie would not have hesitated.

HALLEY:
How do you know?

MICHAEL:
Because I *know*.

HALLEY:
He might have started to hope, just like you did.

MICHAEL:
No way.

HALLEY:
But he sounds like a hopeful person, always running towards everything and cheering for the Toronto Maple Leafs and flying around your room all the time.

MICHAEL:
He flew away. I thought he died—I even phoned his mom to check but she said he was the same.

HALLEY:
…maybe it means he's at peace—that the spirit part of him is at peace because of the story you wrote and now, even though his body is still in acute care, his spirit is free.

MICHAEL:
That's a nice idea but his spirit was probably never here in the first place—it was probably just me thinking about him all the time.

HALLEY:
If Robbie ever gets a little bit of his hearing back and you're far away at war, would you ask his mom if I could come and read to him?

MICHAEL:
See, right there—that is your biggest friggin' problem.

HALLEY:
What?

MICHAEL:
You hope too much.

HALLEY:
And your biggest friggin' problem is that you don't believe that hope is a form of courage and that it is just as honourable—and I do!

MICHAEL:
Well I don't!

HALLEY:
Well I do! I believe that—

MICHAEL:
I don't want to start fighting—I just wanted to give you a thank-you present for coming to read to me!

HALLEY:
...a present?

MICHAEL:
Yeah.

He takes a little white seashell out of his pocket and offers it to her.

...here.

HALLEY:
(takes the shell) Is this your seashell?

MICHAEL:

I'd like you to keep it as a souvenir of us reading together.

HALLEY:

You better keep it—just in case.

MICHAEL:

Just in case what?

HALLEY:

Maybe if you'd had it with you that night there might not have been a big explosion.

MICHAEL:

I had it with me the whole time.

HALLEY:

...you did?

MICHAEL:

Yeah—in the pocket of my flak jacket.

HALLEY:

...oh.

She looks at the seashell in her hand.

MICHAEL:

Stuff like that isn't magic, eh. It's just something to hang on to when everything starts going to rat shit around you.

HALLEY:

I'll put it in the box where I keep special things like my dad's key chain. It even has a lock on it so Clara can't snoop.

Her phone rings again—she clicks it off.

The bus.

MICHAEL:
Guess you better not keep him waiting again.

HALLEY:
I wish I had something to give you.

MICHAEL:
You already gave me lots.

HALLEY:
If you start getting shot at or bombs start falling on you just remember to say the clan motto: *I remain unvanquished.* When I get stuck on a curb and a bike is speeding down the sidewalk towards me I say it to myself and it works *every single* time.

MICHAEL:
All right, but I want you to remember something, too.

HALLEY:
What?

MICHAEL:
I chose this.

HALLEY:
...I know.

MICHAEL:
Goodbye, Halley. Armstrong.

He reaches out to shake her hand. She shakes his hand firmly.

HALLEY:
Goodbye, Corporal Armstrong.

She swivels her wheelchair around, heads towards the door, and exits.

MICHAEL *sits down on the bed. He picks up the pillow and hugs it fiercely against his chest, like a body.*

After a moment he puts the pillow back on the bed. He gets to his feet, walks over to the window, and looks out.

The end.

ACKNOWLEDGEMENTS

I wish to thank Maureen Labonté for her invaluable dramaturgy; Sergeant P.M. "Trapper" Cane, CD, for sharing his experience of being a soldier; Rachel Ditor for her enthusiasm; Kelly Robinson for his support and Mary Blackstone for her play analysis; all the fine actors who did readings along the way; and a big thank you to Neil McPherson, Jennifer Bakst, and Michael Petrasek. I also wish to acknowledge the generous support of the Banff Centre's 75th Anniversary Commissioning program, the Banff Playwrights Colony, and Theatre Arts at The Banff Centre, as well as the support of the Citadel Theatre's Playwrights Forum.

INTERVIEW WITH THE PLAYWRIGHT

As part of this series of plays commissioned by The Banff Centre, we asked each playwright to sit down with another contemporary Canadian playwright for a conversation about their writing lives and the plays that came out of the Centre. Colleen Murphy was interviewed in May 2014 by Judith Thompson, a two-time Governor General's Literary Award–winner and recipient of the prestigious Susan Smith Blackburn Prize. She is the author of such acclaimed plays as The Crackwalker, Palace of the End, *and* White Biting Dog.

JUDITH THOMPSON: So there are two sentences in the wonderful *Armstrong's War* that I thought pertained to your playwriting. One is "Every contact leaves a trace." I really like that. Does the young girl say that or the soldier?

COLLEEN MURPHY: The young girl says that because at some point she said she'd like to be a forensic scientist and she quotes Edmond Locard, who was the father of forensic science, and that's one of his quotes, "Every contact leaves a trace."

JT: It reminded me of Nancy Drew, and even the beginning of the play reminded me of reading my two hundred Nancy Drew books when I was ten years old.

CM: I didn't read Nancy Drew when I was young, but I read a couple to make up this story because I needed to know how they went.

JT: It was a perfect… not even parody. You also understood what draws young girls to it. I wanted to know about the doc and who's in the shack and all that. I thought it was fantastic, and how you created her character through what she's reading.

cm: You probably don't struggle with this any more—and I do less and less—but how do you never have exposition? How do you start in the middle but show something about this young girl, that she's not just any young girl. And how to juxtapose the first impression you might get of her which is, "Oh, this poor girl, she's in a wheelchair."

jt: You completely do that because I even forget she's in a wheelchair.

cm: That's good.

jt: Which I really appreciated because I'm working on a play with people who are wheelchair users and they would appreciate it too. It's just a thing. And the biggest is not walking, it's waiting for the damn Wheel-Trans; you really got that right. But you're never expositional or message-y about it, it's just there. The other sentence I really like is about death, "Death is always your battle."

cm: I think that the stage is one of the few places in the world where you can confront your own death, or others' deaths, and subsequently your own life. Or, how to live your life, how to die, and subsequently how to love. And I think the stage, because it's three-dimensional and everyone is the same scale—the actors on the stage are the same scale as the people in the audience, all breathing the same air—is where we as an audience can confront death. Which makes it to me a most magnificent medium.

jt: Absolutely. And it goes by so fast when somebody does die. There's ceremony and this and that but you are able to isolate it, frame it, and freeze it so we can look at it.

cm: Exactly. Because we're safe from it, we're not losing our family members. We're experiencing the feelings that we've invested into the characters on the stage, but it's safe for us in the sense that we can feel all the feelings but our family's not up there dying.

jt: What motivated this particular play on war?

CM: Well I wanted to write about honour and war, most particularly honour between soldiers. I went and found a soldier who would speak to me. He was not a soldier from Afghanistan; he had been in Bosnia. He was a sniper. He had had an accident and lost his leg. He spoke to me at length and he helped me—I mean, you know this as a playwright, you get a sniff of something and you know it exists but you don't have the experience of it. I couldn't understand what honour means in war. War is a brutal, ugly, bloody thing. So this soldier helped me understand what honour was, and—I say it in the play—it comes down to one thing: your word.

JT: You keep your word.

CM: You keep your word. No matter what. That's why when you're out in war, shooting, you don't turn around and run. In the Roman Empire, one of the reasons that you became a soldier—and you had to be a soldier for so many years—is that you wore this red cloak. Well the red cloak always symbolized blood. And the reason it symbolized blood is that when you were a soldier the blood you drew was honourable. Because you were a soldier.

JT: Right. Defending your country, your women, your children. Is that what *The Red Badge of Courage* is?

CM: *The Red Badge of Courage* is interesting because on some level it's about many things. The reason I was attracted to the book was it seemed to allow the soldier to have his own feelings of what he was going through.

JT: But your writing, the soldier's writing, is so good. I just wrote, "I'm jealous because you can write novels really well too." It was so compelling. I wanted to read the whole book!

CM: Well, thank you. The first one I did in my first few drafts was really, really good, with description coming out the wazoo. It had poetics, description! A playwright friend of mine, Joan MacLeod, read an early, early draft and said, "That's really good. That's too good. He really wouldn't write that good."

JT: But sometimes editing makes things cleaner in a Raymond Carver kind of way, or Ernest Hemingway. And because you edited out all of the poetry, which I'm sure was great, it made it so strong, clean, simple.

CM: So Michael writes this story about a promise he made with his fellow soldier that if either was wounded to a point where they thought they would not live a full life—and it's a hard thing to say, "a full life," because that's subjective—they would kill the other person. Michael writes a story about how he had kept his promise. And to me, it's heroic. He wanted to write a heroic story. One of my favourite lines in the play, he says he smothered his friend. His friend had nothing below his lungs, his legs blown off, he probably would have died anyways, but who knows. The point is no one knows. So he smothers his friend, his friend dies, and he says, "War is not clean—sometimes you have to make it clean." Halley's listening to this lovely story, she admires him, but she thinks it's stupid. And they have the worst fight.

JT: Because she's in a wheelchair. She's saying, "How can you judge what makes a life full?"

CM: She doesn't like the story because she thinks it's wrong. When he writes the story he doesn't put himself in it, but when they're fighting he slips up and says his friend's name. So Halley, who's very smart, picked up on it and is pretty disgusted. They have a fight and she leaves. She comes back—you know, he buys her a bouquet of flowers—because she wants the friggin' badge. She's like, "I will walk through fire to get this friggin' badge." And she doesn't want the flowers, nothing. So she comes back and she's written her version of his story. It's pretty funny.

JT: It's hilarious.

CM: This time she has the soldier live and getting married and all of this stuff and she goes on about the wedding, meanwhile Michael's getting really mad, saying, "Look, it didn't have a happy ending." But through it all she also tells the truth about her own accident, a very ugly car collision in which her father died, very different than what she first tells Michael, this quite lovely ski accident that she could control. She's a lonely girl. She keeps to herself, keeps claiming to have one friend, which she does, but it's clear that the friend uses her for homework and stuff. Somehow Michael and Halley meet in a kind of emotional place, which is an understanding that each of them have gone through some difficulties.

JT: Fate has sort of buffeted them.

CM: In the last scene, because she has told him the truth of her accident, he finds a way to tell her the truth about what happened to his friend Robbie. And you find out, of course, that Robbie's alive. He's deaf, he has brain damage, he's everything, he is there but all you can see from the outside is the breathing machine. I think about this—it's not in the play—but I don't think Michael has gone to see him.

JT: Do they change each other, these two characters?

CM: I think for sure he's changed. And I think she... she is such a— You know, it was so interesting watching the director working with the young girl during the scene with "pick a book from the bag, take a book from the bag," and she's bossing the soldier around. She said to the young girl, "Now you be the captain of the soldier and you order him around." And it was so interesting, right, because both of these characters are in uniform.

JT: Right, she's in her Girl Guides uniform.

CM: She's got her sash that's full of badges.

JT: What's brilliant about that choice is that it's very clear to me that Girl Guides and Boy Scouts were all about wartime, preparing young people to eventually become soldiers and serve in war. And they prepare them really well and that's why it's so unfashionable now too because, in Canada, it's all connected to England. It's Girl Guides instead of Girl Scouts. Were you ever in it?

CM: I was. I was a Brownie. *(raises fingers in salute)* And a Girl Guide. But it was also the notion—because Pathfinders is not in the States—of being able to survive in the woods.

JT: I liked it. She's sort of a junior female soldier. She needs to get her badge. She's maybe being used by her friend but at the beginning she's using him. He's the "poor vet" and she's going to get her badge.

CM: She comes in treating him as if he's a poor vet with PTSD and treating him as a stereotype.

JT: She wants to fit him into the box and he won't fit in. One of the brilliant things about your writing is that the juxtaposition of those two characters is so comical and yet your writing is always just as dark as it is funny. It's such the perfect choice rather than a middle-aged well-meaning lady coming in to help him. There's something about her absolute innocence, but it also reflects the innocent boy that was in him before he went out.

CM: They're very young. I also think that war really affects young people. It affects everybody, but particularly young people because if they survive it they take it into their future. I started this play quite a while ago and it was very hard to write. It took me a long time.

JT: I remember you saying that it's like a perfect vase or something. It's sculpted perfectly.

CM: It took many forms and it had many characters. And it drove me up the friggin' wall.

JT: Why? Tell me how it evolved.

CM: I think I imposed a structure on it and imposed a set of characters on it, like a family. I just assumed it was a family play. And the soldier, Michael, was in his thirties, and he had a friend and the friend had survived. Oh god, I shouldn't even say this but the friend survived but very badly. Basically, after many years, he wanted to come and see Michael and go on a hunting trip. He's a quadriplegic, and he wanted Michael to shoot him in the woods. It was so embarrassing! So embarrassing! I was at Banff when I got this commission and I was so embarrassed and so stuck. It took me forever because I couldn't get it because I had to let go of the structure and the characters.

JT: How did you finally come to this clean, simple structure?

CM: Embarrassment and humiliation! *(laughter)* Halley had been the daughter of one of the soldiers and I quite liked her voice. She was like a raving optimist. And the soldier, I just made him much younger. I understood that it's very hard to put war on the stage.

JT: But you're really astute at finding the angle to write from. In *The December Man* it's the aftermath [of the École Polytechnique massacre]—one of the men who survived kills himself, and then his parents kill themselves, so you wrote about that. You were right in the heart of the massacre at Polytechnique by writing about how it resonated.

CM: Off to the side.

JT: But brings us closer to the centre than if you had women lined up because we almost can't do that, and that's what you're doing here too. We might as well be in the trenches.

CM: Well I also thought at the core of this is the notion of mercy killing in war. To write about that… it's a hard thing to write about right on.

JT: You've never been there, but you address that in a metatheatrical way in the moment it's revealed that Stephen Crane was never at war. And yet it undeniably works. We as playwrights have never been in a lot of situations we write about but we have to have a sense whether we have an internal or mystical permission to go there, and you have.

CM: I was very cognizant of humour. It's "funny" that allows people to relax into some of the darkness. It's a dark ending. The second last scene, the penultimate scene, that's really where the big reveal is. That's where things should go and your last scene is a different kind of normalcy because it's drama not a tragedy, but that's where I fought really hard structurally because once I had gotten the characters, the idea of the play, trying to figure out how to put the big reveal in the last scene, about two minutes away from the end of the play, that's what I fought with for quite a long time. And I realized it just could not go in that second last scene because then the last scene would be a goodbye scene and I would risk sentimentalizing all that had gone before.

JT: And you have not done that at all. Just looking at my notes I'm remembering now "I remain unvanquished." Is that a Girl Guide or Pathfinder—

CM: No, it's actually the Armstrong's clan motto!

JT: Oh! The Armstrong's clan motto. Is it Halley who knows it or him? I can't remember.

CM: It's Halley. Her grandmother tells her when she's first in a wheelchair and being teased at school, "This is what you say to yourself, you use it as both a shield and a sword."

JT: It's beautiful. All these little phrases you have throughout resound like poetry at the centre and make us think about what that means. In war, we are unvanquished or we are vanquished, and what does it mean, as human beings, if I lose my legs. Am I vanquished? I imagine that I would be but I know from working with my wheelchair performers that I wouldn't be.

CM: You wouldn't be and you know you wouldn't be, I think. I think you know that. I think I know that too.

JT: Although it's our greatest fear, isn't it? Maybe blindness or that? Quadriplegia? Beyond our children.

CM: Blindness would do me in.

JT: That's what I feel too.

CM: Everything to me, even writing, is visual. For me, I never hear nothing. I never hear a boo. Everything is visual.

JT: Well you're a filmmaker too.

CM: Even how the writing goes on the page and where the shape of the words are. That's playwriting for me.

JT: Do you see the set when you write?

CM: I see it to some extent, not as a concrete... but I see things in a three-dimensional space.

JT: So you imagine his bed...

CM: I imagine his bed.

JT: ...and what he looks like?

CM: No, never what he looks like. But I always knew that the first image of the play would be a dark room, the bed a freakin' mess, sheets hanging down to the floor, and all you see is a foot, a bare foot. Then the door opens and you see this girl in a wheelchair, you see this light coming into the dark room, but that's the whole play. The guy's dead, he's in his coffin, and she opens the door and some light comes in the room. That, to me, states in one image the story, because you just have to take that image to its logical extreme. She opens the coffin.

JT: She's youth, she's resolve, she remains unvanquished...

CM: And she wants her freakin' badge.

JT: And she wants her badge.

CM: And she'll drag you out of your coffin to get it. So those kinds of images are what come to me.

JT: Getting lost in art can almost fill us with despair—the sickness unto death, the whole Kierkegaard kind of thing—the brownie points and getting badges, it pulls us out.

CM: She's on the cusp of puberty. One of the reasons I made her not in puberty—these young girls, they're just amazing, right? And they really can take on the world no matter what and can change the world. I have to say at times I just wanted to take a big sponge baseball bat and beat her over the head. And I thought, "Oh god, will people just hate her?"

JT: No, they love her, and the fact that she's annoying is part of the comedy.

CM: Yeah, I had to allow her to be annoying to the audience.

JT: Oh it's wonderful, it's just such an unexpected duo. And you're right, if she had hit puberty, that's when girls start to lose their self-esteem no matter how beautiful they are and it's all self-consciousness and it's all a different game and he would have to fight his attraction to her and all that stuff would go on. And that's probably what he hoped for when he signed up for the reader, an attractive seventeen-year-old. But then he gets an annoying twelve-year-old. She's so funny! There are certain things I wrote down, I love it when she says, "No one can see the future—not even fortune tellers." It's like she's just realized that and is quite proud of realizing it. In these notes I described some of the details that I really loved. "Robbie, Robbie... rest your head." So Robbie's under Michael's bed.

CM: Well this is the third character in the play but he's not real. He's the spirit of Robbie, who's in the room with Michael from the beginning, but when Michael reads the story that he's written, the spirit of Robbie disappears. You could take that many ways. To write this story liberates him to some extent.

JT: From the ghost. The ghost of a person who's alive but also the ghost of not keeping his word.

CM: I think it's a terrible guilt. Again, it's not stated because you could play that in different ways. The older actor at Finborough, he's on the bed weeping, it just tore your heart out. There's a level of guilt and then it disappears. It's not that cut and dry but he can't get the spirit back. And then he says at the end, "His spirit was probably never here in the first place—it was probably just me thinking about him all the time." But he treats him like a corporeal body.

JT: Is that one of the essences of this play, how do we live if we betray our own ethical self or truth? If we break our word, how do we live with it?

CM: I think it's a question in the play, how do we live with it? But then I think what Halley does in a weird way, and this is me interpreting my own work, is push all the way to the end. Michael says he couldn't kill him, "I started to hope; I couldn't help it," and she says, at the very end when they start fighting again, "Your biggest friggin' problem is that you don't believe that hope is a form of courage and that it is just as honourable—and I do!" She's on to something there.

JT: Do your personal issues ever really enter into your writing? Like me, you don't really write biographically ever, but something, some blood is on the page at the same time. Have you ever broken your word?

CM: I consider myself a pretty strong existentialist; I believe that one must take responsibility for every moment of one's life and therefore everything one utters. But I'm sure I have in the past. If I break my word I try to own up to it.

JT: Have you ever done anything that you continue to feel guilty about or haunts you, or is that all resolved in your head?

CM: I try to work through that stuff because I can easily be haunted by it, consumed by it.

JT: We must wrestle with this because we can pretend to make them go away but they won't.

CM: The ghosts are the ghosts are the ghosts.

JT: Yeah, they're there and Halley comes and forces Michael to confront them and wrestle with them, and then her own ghost, which is her accident and her lying about the accident. Is she changed by him, by her interaction with him?

CM: She goes through quite a sobering experience, and an adult experience. And she doesn't know about war and she admits it. Her world has expanded somewhat. So I think that's what she takes away. There's an openness in her world view—and it may not land. For both these characters it doesn't land at the end of the play. It lands later. The one good thing that he says at the end of the play, which kind of puts everything in place for him, is, "I want you to remember something, too… I chose this." He's saying he chose to go to war.

JT: Why did he choose to go to war?

CM: Because he believed that he was going to help people. People say you go to war so that others don't have to. Soldiers go to war because they get sent but you have to ask why soldiers become soldiers. What do they want out of it? Many believe that they are joining a situation in which they will make a contribution to the world. Just the way somebody would say, "I'm going to be a social worker, I'm going to make a contribution to the world." When Michael talks in the play about the war, he's not painting a very pretty picture of it, not a very patriotic picture, if you want to use that term. He's painting a realistic picture. He says, "Why should the Afghan people believe we're there to help them?" And he says, "There never was going to be a victory." And this is set in 2007 when there were a lot of surges by the Canadians at that time. But this young guy, he's seen quite a bit, he's saying "Nobody's gonna win."

JT: There was a documentary somebody made and the Canadian soldiers admitted to the filmmaker, "I hate all of them, I hate every Afghan man, woman, and child." I thought that was very brave filmmaking; we're sending them with the idea that they're helping. So the only honour they can have when they realize there's no honour in the war is between each other.

CM: I spoke to one soldier in depth and his experience was not in Afghanistan but he's very, very active with all the vets. He gave me a glimpse, and I would only ever say a glimpse. The character of Michael in this war, it's a narrow view of honour. And I needed to contain it because this isn't an anti-war play. It's not a war play either. Well, it's about war but it's not an anti-war play. What I tried to sustain, without sentimentalizing and romanticizing, is the notion of a soldier. A soldier who believes in what he does and has a conscience about doing it. Or not doing it.

JT: What draws you to a soldier, to war?

CM: I don't really know. I just know that I've always read so much on Napoleon and the Romans… I studied a lot of the Roman Empire. So much of what we see today is from the Roman Empire. It was a hugely militaristic empire that extended from North Africa to England. You look at the Greeks, you look at war, for men, it's like their period. *(laughter)*

JT: Really?

CM: That's where they bleed!

JT: Or like childbirth.

CM: Like childbirth. I love tension and drama and life-and-death stakes, and you get very high stakes in war. I remember watching the battle in Eisenstein's film *Alexander Nevsky*, "The Battle on the Ice," and he was shooting this during the second world war in some studio with cardboard for ice and you think, "This is horrible, this is terrible, war, people are dying, and I love it!" So operatic. I don't know why I like war.

JT: Roméo Dallaire said in an interview, "Let's not kid around, those moments on the battlefield, there is nothing more exciting, it's a thousand times even better than sex and if anybody tells you that's not true they're lying to you."

CM: You're damn right. And I think that war and all the things that go with it are far more complex than just saying "I'm against it" or "I'm for it." It's a complex dance that uses a great deal of our human impulses.

JT: As a very political being, I admire that this is apolitical and focused. But do you feel you've betrayed yourself at all by not being political in the play and not taking a stand against the war?

CM: I think that I offer to the audience the ability to make a decision. I can't make the decision in the play, otherwise it's just a pamphlet. There were some performances where people were very, very upset and they were moved—not that they didn't appreciate the humour, but deeply upset.

JT: Why were they upset?

CM: Just the stuff conjured up in them about war. Perhaps they had relatives. But I see plays, a play like this, as a conjuring stick—it conjures up stuff in the audience. If you dig deep enough in this play there's my perspective, but it's fluid.

JT: I see it there. It's almost like war happened to him for really no reason and what happened to her is the same, the car accident. An accident.

CM: There is a randomness, a terrible randomness, in life. But do I see this play as apolitical? I don't know. I don't think it lacks politics but I don't think that it puts its politics anywhere in the foreground. What I'm learning, as I write more plays, is that I always go in through the character and I can only offer up whatever to the audience through the character. So the audience have to respond to the character in their situation. I think the audience can change their minds a few times during the course of a reasonably short play. So that's all I can offer and they go away thinking about it.

JT: War is the ultimate test of character, they say. And they point out some quiet guy who no one notices and he's this huge hero in World War Two who saved whole troops. That's where we're tested.

CM: We spend our whole life, daily life, protecting ourselves from getting killed, right, crossing the street, driving along the 401. In war you have to say very consciously, "I am going to stand in front of people who want to kill me."

And the experiential feeling of putting yourself in harm's wary and getting shot at puts you in a situation that you can never come back from. Soldiers understand that amongst themselves. I can imagine it. To put yourself there, even if it's only once, you have to leave a part of you there. It's such a heightened experience. You are an atom away from life and death and that's what you experience at that moment. It's part terrific, terrific excitement and part overwhelming fear. What do you do with that experience?

JT: They want to get away and get home more than anything all the time, and more than anything they want to go back.

CM: In one piece.

JT: In one piece. "Later Aidan would lie in bed wondering what the swallows saw." That's just beautiful.

CM: There are swallows in Afghanistan.

JT: Those details!

CM: Halley uses it later when she talks about the real thing that happened to her, the terrible thing. The car lying sideways in the ditch. And she says, "You know how in your story you had swallows looking down?... well, if birds were looking down they would have seen two humans lying in a ditch and a car lying sideways behind a small person with pink legs and a large person in a suit." That's her. The swallows bring the perspectives together. But you don't think of that at the time.

JT: To go back to "Death is always your battle, how we face death is who we are," and how Halley says, "My stepfather says." Details like that, she has a stepfather, is that important, random, or how would you describe that, your choice there?

CM: I had to figure out the mother, how the father died, that he didn't die right away when he was in the ditch, that he suffered a lot for three days, and Halley felt terribly in the family, and she overheard her mother speaking on the phone and saying to a friend, "The best thing about this terrible situation was that he lived long enough to say goodbye to me." But then Halley got upset because the mother married after a year and it was hard on Halley—she was very, very close to her father. As playwrights we have a complete life behind these characters. You use a word like stepfather and it says it already.

JT: Her feelings about her father and wishing her father could have lived even in that terrible state, kids do that. I remember having dreams that my dad, who died of cancer, had wires hooked up to him and was living in the closet, and I'd be so happy. "Oh you're here, you've been here all along. Fantastic!" And I'd wake up and he was still dead. I think a kid—not an adult who doesn't want anyone to live in pain—even in that horrible state in the hospital, would wish their father was still there. Whether consciously or unconsciously, you've drawn an emotional wire from that into her feeling about Robbie. Why would you let him die? He could have lived, and if only my dad could have lived. It's so complicated, what you've done.

CM: She says every time that she talks about the skiing story, which is her fake story about the accident, that it's about control, but really it's about the fact that in the skiing story her dad's still alive.

JT: I read a lot of plays on juries, from students, and a kind of theatrical crackling quality is missing is so many of them, the musicality of the back and forth. Does that come to you automatically or do you do that through sculpting or reading out loud?

CM: It's partly visual. Because of how the words look. That sounds weird. I have to thank my musical training because it's all about the engine, the rhythm. And because I look at everything visually I can actually see the rhythm play out in the shape of the words. But then I also do a metronome—not a real one—a (*sounds out a beat*).

JT: Inside. I think I do too. And that's when dialogue fails, when it's not there.

CM: And it's an easy test. It's an engine, an internal rhythm almost.

JT: And conflict helps. When people are in conflict they gain that rhythm. Right now we're not in conflict so it's probably arrhythmic. We're just really trying to communicate but if we had to do a test we'd probably make it rhythmic.

CM: Oh yeah. Because it's all music.

JT: What does death mean to you?

CM: Oblivion.

JT: Death is oblivion, there's no afterlife.

CM: No. It's the dirt.

JT: You grew up Catholic? Is that in your plays at all?

CM: It's going to be in my new play. It's about an Irish Catholic family.

JT: What's the play about—is it partly biographical?

CM: It's sort of my dad's family. Potato farmers in PEI, Irish Catholic. It's called *O'Brian Road*.

JT: Really? Do they have a road? O'Brian Road?

CM: Murphy Road.

JT: Do they have a Murphy Road?

CM: They do.

JT: They have a Thompson Road here too, in Belmont. So you're going down O'Brian Road and one day I'll go down Thompson Road.

CM: This is a big play, but I'm trying to make it so it's not close to me. What I'm looking at, in the play, is through the lens of family but divided by loyalties of nationalism and religion. That's what I'm looking at.

JT: Does it take place in Ireland or PEI?

CM: It takes place in PEI.

JT: So nationalism: Canadian...

CM: Politically Canadian and politically Irish. And religion, the Catholics and the East Coast. In a play religion enchants us. It enchants us as it deceives us. I've always wanted to write about religion without having it be a rant.

JT: People need it. And people want it. And thank god for it, for the community, for shut-ins being brought to church, all that kind of thing, for good works. It's undeniable. And bad works, trying to convert people and everything. Just community. That's a good thing. People gathering together and trying to be spiritual. I suppose that's what we're doing in some ways, but then there are the terrible rules and laws.

CM: Well there are no rules and laws on the stage. I say the stage is a country without borders and flags and you can bring anything to it. You can bring your paradise to it, your trauma.

JT: I always ask myself, and students, what taboos have you broken? Where have you transgressed? That's the only reason for a play to exist is if you're transgressing. Not in order to shock, but because it's true. Because it's there.

CM: I think the stage will outlive all the technical and digital advances. It's very powerful. It'll go through its ups and downs, its trouble getting audiences. I mean, it's been around for—yesterday was World Theatre Day—the stage has been around for 2,500 years. And we're sitting here talking about it. It has tremendous conjuring ability.

JT: And why? I wrote a chapter for a book called *Why Theatre Now?* So I put that question to Facebook and I got a lot of answers that one would expect, but Seana McKenna gave a nice answer that theatre is now.

CM: It's the immediate.

JT: And only now. Somebody else gave a lovely answer in my class, that theatre never dates, good theatre. Whereas a film made in '78 looks like a film made in '78 and you love it for that era.

CM: The great films don't date. But there are many, many things you have to have in place to make a great film. The thing about theatre is that you experience it so immediately, even if you're looking at a play from Euripides.

JT: They can't polish it up, there's no polishing it, no editing.

CM: Because theatre's about feeling. I think the audience and the actors meet in the land of the theatre, and they go through that emotional experience each night together.

JT: I wonder if different cultures that are outwardly emotional—our culture's so repressed emotionally that it's a great gift to be able to experience emotional reality for two hours—in Italy or places where people seem to be less repressed, have their own form of repression.

CM: Well with Italy there's opera, which is such a great medium.

JT: But the theatre's not great there, actually.

CM: But look at opera there! The opera is, as a form, closer to Greek tragedy than any other form surviving in the current day.

JT: But you're writing that. You're writing Greek tragedy, in a sense.

CM: Yeah, I like it. I like the form. This isn't. (*pointing to* Armstrong's War)

JT: But what you wrote with *Pig Girl* was Greek tragedy. It all happened off stage. They thought *Pig Girl* was too much or whatever, but you dared to put horror on the stage.

CM: That's more the Roman model. At the Colosseum.

JT: At the Colosseum, of course, but that was for entertainment and you are not doing it for entertainment.

CM: It wasn't just for entertainment, no. It was a tremendous amount of ritual to appease the gods and all kinds of psychological notions, that you can make people courageous and fearless by having them watch people die.

JT: Whoa, really?

CM: There were all kinds of things in the Colosseum.

JT: So that, the gladiators and all that was about making the audience fearless?

CM: Yeah, the audience watches people die and they become fearless. It's all pretty horrible.

JT: But isn't that what Afghanistan is in a way? Our children go out and die for a so-called cause and does that make us fearless as a nation, or give us the reputation?

CM: That's a good question because we live in one of the most fearful times. I'm saying this off the cuff, but we live in such a climate of total fear—I don't know if it's just post-9/11—and greed comes from fear, fear of the unknown.

JT: We're afraid of confronting ourselves and that's why everyone is on their cellphones all the time.

CM: Fear of silence, fear of reflection.

JT: You cannot walk alone because you have to be alone with your thoughts, your regrets, your ghosts.

CM: We project fear into everything, into our children.

JT: As a young girl I was scared of everything. Not in my writing and not when it came to my children, and only in the last ten years have I discovered fearlessness. It was in the writing but not in me. I think you've always been fearless. You don't care what people think.

CM: No, but that's taken a long time to get to that point. I mean, I do care. I gotta make a buck, I gotta pay the rent. I do care, but theatre is an exciting place and I need to challenge myself. I have feelings about the world I live in and things that happen in the world and I feel compelled to write about them.

JT: And that is the way you serve because you're a master playwright and that's your service. You were a guide for your late husband, Allan King, and he was a guide for you as well. What did he learn from you and what did you learn from him? In the play there are all these wonderful wisdoms like "My dad said the word 'try' is an escape route." I just love that because we know that when someone says they'll try to get to your play they're not coming.

CM: That's Allan.

JT: Is that Allan? I love it that I got that!

CM: That's really good because, holy smokes, he would say exactly that. He would say, "You're not going to try, you're going to do. Try means you're not really going to do, just sort of maybe do."

JT: What did he learn from you?

CM: I don't know... I still have a very difficult time talking about him. I still can't even take off my wedding ring. There was a great age difference between us but it never felt so. From the day I met him we talked about having this affinity between us. An affinity. And so I learned how to take authority for my decisions from him and how to stand behind myself.

JT: Because he made the documentaries he made and they were tough and out there.

CM: He was a tough guy. We were very close. Very close. So we learned a lot from each other. I can't believe that you pulled that right out of my play!

JT: What's the final word, the final thoughts you'd like to offer on the play *Armstrong's War*?

CM: That it's a journey. It's a journey for these two characters, for the audience. To think about war, honour, courage, and hope.

JT: And what would you offer to young playwrights learning to write by reading your play? What did you learn as a playwright? You learn something, I think, with the writing of every play. What did you learn as a playwright?

CM: It takes an enormous amount of perseverance. This took me five years. My husband was ill in the middle of it and he died and my life fell apart, but that's not the only reason why it took so long. It took so long because I couldn't get at the material. I'm always amazed that I finally got at the material, through these characters. I think what I want to say to young playwrights is that you have to write and write and write and don't go soliciting advice. Just write the fucker.

JT: And just keep going. You could have given up in five years. Many people would have just given up.

CM: Well sometimes you don't know the shape it's going to take. And you can't go around asking people to tell you the shape it should take. You have to discover the shape it's going to take by writing it and just persevering.

JT: Did you write other plays in the meantime?

CM: Yeah, I was working on *The Goodnight Bird*.

JT: But this kept calling you back.

CM: I was so humiliated because I had been given money from The Banff Centre.

JT: Oh yes! We're good citizens aren't we? We're given money, we damn well finish it.

CM: It's been given money and a Leighton Colony and a Playwrights' Colony and I was out there but all, "Oh, I can't do a reading because my play's not ready." I'd go back to my room thinking, "I can't believe it. I've got this piece of shit here and I don't know what to do with it."

JT: *(laughs)* That gives hope to young playwrights. Keep going.

CM: It reads well now!

Colleen Murphy is an award-winning author who was born in Rouyn-Noranda, Quebec, and lives in Toronto. Her plays include *The December Man (L'homme de décembre)*—winner of the 2007 Governor General's Literary Award for Drama, the Carol Bolt Award, and the Alberta Theatre Projects Enbridge playRites Award—*Pig Girl, Beating Heart Cadaver, The Goodnight Bird,* and *The Piper,* among others. She is also a librettist (*The Enslavement and Liberation of Oksana G.*) and an award-winning filmmaker whose distinct films have played in festivals around the world. For more information, visit www.colleenmurphy.ca.